ROOT DOWN
And
RISE UP

TURN YOUR SETBACK INTO YOUR COMEBACK

With love &light Always! Kim ♡

BY KIMBERLY REID

Published by Kimberly Reid
ISBN: 978-0-692-15476-2 (Paperback)

Printed in the United States of America

Book Cover Design, Interior Design, Typesetting, and Pre-press Production: Amber Hargett

TABLE OF CONTENTS

"Honest. Vulnerable. Relatable. Kim's accessible storytelling style allows readers to make sense, and more importantly, make MEANING from her life experience. Come rest and share your energy with your new friend, Kim Reid. Read and know that you are not alone, and that you have everything you need to blossom fully into YOU! Be renewed and bolstered with Root Down and Rise Up."

- Elizabeth J. Warner, MD FACP CPE,
President, Warner Well Being

Acknowledgements

Thank you God for working through me, allowing me to serve as a messenger of light and hope to others for a higher and greater good.

To begin, I acknowledge YOU, my reader. Thank you for your willingness to pick up this book and read it with an open mind and open heart taking with you what you need. I am grateful for your support and allowing me to share a part of my journey with you. Thank you.

To my loving parents, Gary and Linda. Thank you for your wisdom, guidance, support, and most of all, your unconditional love and grace through one of the most heartbreaking times of my adult life.

Mindy, Sheri, Andrea, Chris, Kevin, and Doug, thank you for always having an open door, having my back, and for gifting me a fresh start with the opportunities that divinely found their way to me.

To my brilliant and dedicated coach and editor, Alisia Leavitt. I am eternally grateful our paths crossed. I am blessed beyond measure with your kindness, professionalism, wit, and honesty throughout this process. Thank you for your leadership, expertise, mentorship, and friendship.

Amber Rochelle-Hargett, thank you for your vision, creativity, and excellence in cover and internal design. Thank you for the care and attention to detail every step of the way.

Thank you to my dear friend and dynamite photographer, Kim Myers. You have a true gift of seeing deep into the lens. You see and feel the story behind it so perfectly. Thank you for capturing mine.

Jason, thank you for your encouragement, compassion, and love. I am grateful for your part in my journey.

Jack and Max…you are my everything. I love you.

When you are down to nothing,
God is up to something.

- Proverbs 16:9

INTRODUCTION

In early 2015, I received disturbing news at work. I had just returned from my lunch break when my boss called me to his office and proceeded to inform me I was being demoted from my management position. As I sat across the desk from him reading the letter that served as the official 30-day notice of my demotion, I was devastated. This news hit me hard, more so than any other traumatic life event I had experienced up to that point. It was one of those moments that made you feel as though you left your body momentarily. My career had always been a huge piece of my identity and who I am, and right before me, it was being stripped away.

I was approaching my 15 year anniversary in public human services. I had spent the last seven years serving as a first line manager. Prior to that, I was a caseworker that assisted individuals and families by processing applications for state aid and assistance benefits. The State department I worked for underwent massive budget cuts, not thinking that our staffing would be impacted. I was wrong. I was caught in the middle of corporate downsizing. In the public sector, it's referred to as a Reduction In Force (RIF). My profession as a manager was abolished and in turn I was involuntarily demoted.
Early in my career, I knew I wanted to move into leadership. I craved more knowledge, more depth to my job, more challenge, more meaning, to not only help the clients I was serving, but also helping my co-workers seek out ways to achieve that. I embrace leadership and being that person who helps others achieve success. I was extremely proud of my job as a case manager and truly enjoyed the work I did serving our clients, and was even more excited to become a manager and continue along the path of leading others to their fullest potential.

I had worked so hard over the course of my career by returning to school in the evenings to earn a higher degree to be able to move upward in my organization. I put in countless extra hours with no compensation. I volunteered for various special projects that I willingly took on as my own reveling in the creative process to help make our organization better. I missed events with my friends because I worked late hours. I sacrificed time spent with my family because of my dedication to my career. What was most bothersome, was that I missed seeing my infant crawl for the first time because I was busy working mandatory overtime on a Saturday during a system upgrade. I did it because I truly believed I was contributing to an organization that cared about me just as much as I cared for it and our mission. Sadly, the harsh truth hit me in January of 2015 as I read my demotion letter. All of the extra time and work I poured into my career meant very little now. Simply because of an archaic civil service rule that determined seniority was more valuable than performance. I felt extremely hurt, rejected, and most of all, I felt blindsided by my organization. I always had faith that my one constant in life was my career because it was a huge piece of who I was. My trust had now been betrayed and I could feel myself start to unravel quickly. I was replaced by another peer who simply had more years of service than me. Just like that my position was eliminated. In the blink of an eye, with the swipe of a pen, a signature approving budget cuts, sealed my fate as I moved from my corner office into a cubicle in the middle hallway.

I sat in stillness many times thinking about the high-performance ratings I had earned over the years. I was so proud of myself and the work I was doing and felt even more fulfilled that my boss recognized and valued my work too. It wasn't right that I was being demoted. Nothing about this situation was okay. I was scared. I didn't know what was going to happen to me or how I would get through this, emotionally, mentally, or financially. It was a helpless feeling that I wasn't at all familiar with. I felt vulnerable that every move I made would be watched or any conversation I had would be judged by my peers on how I was going to handle this.

I began an inward journey of processing the news and feelings surrounding my demotion. I had become lost and felt unsupported in my work. I didn't feel valued or that my purpose for being a leader was either appreciated or noticed. However, these were my own internal projections of how I was feeling towards myself. I had lost the drive to try something new and innovative. The creativity had dwindled and escaped me.

This wasn't a reflection of my boss, this was a reflection of me. I created that internal story and continued to project those feelings to the point that they finally manifested themselves into my demotion. I had no one to blame but myself.

Often, we become caught up in our own methods of doing things at our jobs that when we experience change, it throws us off and has us feeling like we are starting over again. That was what I experienced with my demotion. I was so caught up in the way I was doing my work and becoming in a complacent frame of mind of just being rather than doing. I could slowly begin to feel the desire escape my spirit. The passion wasn't there any longer, the drive had long left me. I didn't feel connected to my purpose or my personal mission of serving others, which was bothersome, but I felt too tired to try and sort it out and get back on track.

Instead, I shifted into this mindset of resentment, judgment, an attitude of having to, rather than wanting to. Somewhere along the way, the spirit of helping others had long left me. It was frustrating to be in a place of not wanting to help anyone around you because of your own unhappiness and reflection from your internal world. What you reflect outward is what you receive back.

Processing my emotions in the days and weeks that followed my demotion was all over the place. I didn't know which end was up. I was lost, embarrassed, hurt, scattered, and scared. In some ways, it felt as though karma was making itself known to me by the unhappiness I was feeling and coming right back to put me in my place. I spent many days experiencing feelings ranging from anger and responsibility to appreciation for still having a position and a paycheck. I maintained firm belief that this wouldn't be how the story ended. My co-worker, Mindy, who was our office manager, checked in on me regularly. She would often stop by my cubicle to say hi, and see how I was feeling. Mindy is one of the most non- judgmental people I know and always offered a listening and supportive ear. Mindy always knew what to say and somehow always found the right words to make you feel better if you were having a bad day. Sometimes she wouldn't have to say anything and instead offered a hug, which sometimes spoke more loudly than any words could. Mindy and I had a great relationship.

About a month after my demotion, I went into work feeling very bitter about my situation even though I had been making intentional efforts to maintain a positive demeanor, but we are human and our emotions can creep up on us anytime. I tried to shake it before I pulled into the parking lot, but

I could still feel the irritation in my stomach. As I trudged through the snow on the sidewalk and approached the back door of our building, I could see the light on in my old office and it triggered a jealous feeling.

Like. Right. Now. Pissed off.com

No one was in the office; the light was simply on as an indicator someone had intended to occupy the space and that someone wasn't me. My emotions got the better of me and they reared their ugly head. I came in the back door and walked into the breakroom where I saw Mindy pouring a cup of coffee. She looked over at me and greeted with me a smile. I looked back at her but couldn't find the smile to return to her, which made me incredibly upset and sad because that's not who I am. She knew my hurt and while I didn't have to say anything to let her know I was upset, my words starting spewing everywhere and I didn't hold back. It wasn't even 8:15 and I was already dropping the F-bomb like it was the word the. I don't even know why I was upset, I just knew I was. Every emotion that I had been processing came out of my mouth in the breakroom that morning and poor Mindy was on the receiving end of it.

After a few moments of hearing how crazy I sounded, I stopped and could feel my eyes fill with tears and a huge lump in my throat. She placed her coffee cup down on the table and walked over to me and gently gave me a hug. I stood there as she hugged me feeling a sense of support, concern, and most of all, validation. I wiped my tears and we walked out of the breakroom together parting ways at the copier as we headed toward our work stations. Later that afternoon, I returned from my break and found a small book on my chair. It was a pocket size devotional book by Joyce Meyer. Mindy was a huge Joyce Meyer fan and had seen her speak live. There was a sticky note with a message written in Mindy's handwriting.

It read: *This book has helped me in many ways and in many times. I hope it might do the same for you.*

I opened it read the first few pages, and couldn't put it down. I blew right thought it and felt my energy shift once I closed the book. I felt renewed, like I had been reunited with a long-lost friend. It was time to go home and as I walked out of the office that day, I was in a different place mentally and emotionally than where I was 8 hours before walking into the building that morning. I felt a strong sense of faith and belief that the outcome for my situation would be positive, even though I had no idea how, when, or what that looked like. I had worked too hard over the last 15 years building my career, serving others, and there was no way this was going to be how my story ended. I had high expectations of myself. I had even higher expectations of God.

Sooner or later, you cool down from being a hot mess to collect your brilliant mind, get your shit together, and prepare to become fierce again. From that point forward, I turned to what I know and lean on when despair and devastation hit. I turned inward to my spirituality. By leaning on my faith and listening to my heart and inner guidance, I applied the methods and lessons I learned throughout this book, that led me to the greatest change in my professional and personal circumstances in my career months later.

Through the process of leaning on faith and reverence, I began to notice a powerful shift in the way I thought about and approached my situation each day. I became aware of my mindset and the enormous role my faith played a part in noticing how I was feeling, by not allowing myself to stay in destructive negative thought patterns. With each new phase of my journey, I found myself learning ways to effectively manage my emotions. Through the principles of reiki, practicing yoga and meditation, running, creating vision boards, journaling, and the ultimate power of prayer, I taught myself new coping mechanisms that not only worked, but turned out to be some of the most valuable tools I still use today when disappointment strikes and life gets messy.

My faith, relationship with God, and the peaceful energy I feel when I pray is my epicenter. I feel closest to spirit when I am experiencing hurt, sadness, and grief, alongside the feelings of joy, exuberance, gratitude, and happiness. I trust that what is intended for my harm, the Universe will use for my good. Sitting in my cubicle after reading that devotional, I was brought back to spirit through my co-worker, and leaned strongly into my faith asking to be shown the way.

The lessons, steps, and conversations spoken from the heart that are shared throughout this book were the answers that came to me by silencing my mind and allowing loving and supportive energy to work through me. These steps are ones I have further developed to help me go through and overcome one of the biggest career challenges I have ever faced. These are my go-to methods and I still use them today when tough situations present themselves. By utilizing and practicing these steps, I discovered a spiritual healing and was introduced to new ways of healing which was an incredible gift to be awakened to.

My intention for this book:

I wrote this book with holding a vision of one person in mind. For the person who hustles with heart and shows up each day because she chooses to and wants to, not because she has to. It is for the person who intentionally commits to building his life by adding layers of opportunities, experience, growth, expansion, wisdom, creativity, and embracing the changes that he goes through and grows through. For the person who found herself back at the start line part-way through the race because life took a different path than what was planned or intended, yet unequivocally knowing there is more meaning and depth than what is on the surface. For the person who sacrificed her own needs to make sure everyone around her was the priority and taken care of, being all things to everyone, at all times, except herself. For the person who has grown complacent in his role and seeking fulfillment, starving for connection, challenge and purpose. For the person who experienced a setback so deep and personal that hurts like hell and wonders how he will ever make it through. Perhaps the description of this person is someone you know all too well. Perhaps this person is you.

Whatever your situation may be, a setback, a break-up, a loss, rejection, or a demotion, there was a reason that you picked up this book and if you have read this far, please accept my invitation to continue this journey with me as I share with you the hurts, the fears, the lessons, the answered prayers, the miracles, the celebrations, and most of all, the rise after the fall.

The idea for this book was fostered on day three of my bump after searching endlessly through pages of on-line content that offered little to no guidance on how to bounce back from adversity with resiliency. Feeling that there was nothing that could offer me comfort and insight I needed on how to handle my adverse situation, I made a promise to myself that I would write a book, not knowing what my outcome would be, what path or opportunities would come my way, if I remained with the same employer or leaving my organization altogether. I made a commitment to share my story in an effort to help another person go through theirs. No one should have to do this alone. Not me. And certainly not you.

The best wisdom and words of encouragement I received were from my boss just days before my demotion became official. He came to my office and took a seat on the outdoor garden bench that decorated my office. He knew my days were limited. He had stopped by a few times each week to visit and update me on any news he learned of regarding the RIF. He was sincere in his manner that there was nothing more he could do other than offer his love and unconditional support. He had truly exhausted all of his efforts in preventing my demotion from happening.

He gently began to tell me the story of the Rise of the Phoenix. He spoke softly with deliberate care and intention as he described the Greek mythology legend of a magical bird, the Phoenix, known for its vibrancy and strength that lived several hundred years before it consumed itself in fire to miraculously rise again in renewal from its own ashes. I knew exactly where he was going with the story. It was a representation of a piece of my career journey that died and was burning, but through faith, perseverance, strength and vibrancy, there would be a rise and renewal from my ashes. He quietly looked down and said that he didn't know exactly how or when that would happen for me, but he knew in his heart that like the Phoenix, I would someday rise again.

He looked up at me with tears in his eyes and patted me on the hand softly. As he left my office, he turned around and wiped his eyes from under his glasses as he said with conviction, "This will only destroy you if you let it." The manner in which he told me that story remains with me as I wrote this book, because in some respect, it was the only thing I held onto for hope and determination to rise again.

At the end of each chapter, I have created an opportunity for you to recognize and reflect on your own experiences and apply the principles and methods described within to help with your comeback. You may want to keep a small notebook or journal available to help with these reflection questions and to write down anything else that may rise to the surface as you go through the chapters.

In yoga practice, during a Sun Salutation, the alignment principle is to become grounded to the floor to be rooted in your pose before rising, to gain awareness, insight and strength, before drawing in a deep breath, lifting the head, and standing up. It is through my personal journey and experience I went through that I share with you the lessons I learned to root down and rise up.

When you are down to nothing,
God is up to something.

- Proverbs 16:9

Chapter One

ROOT DOWN:
SURRENDER TO THE UNIVERSE'S PLAN

A s my laptop clock turned from 4:59 to 5:00 pm on Friday, February 13th, 2015, I knew it was real. My demotion was official. It had been a month since my boss had called me into his office and gave me the news. I looked out my office window and watched my co-workers leave the building for the weekend. My gaze turned away from the window and back to my computer screen hoping to see a last minute e-mail come through from the Governor's Office containing an order rescinding all layoffs and demotions.

5:01 pm, and no further e-mail.

I began to delete the voicemails I had saved, along with the history of incoming calls. I mindlessly kept hitting the delete button with each number that popped up, until January 16, 2015 and the name of my boss appeared. I stopped and realized it was the day I received the call from him asking me to come and see him.

Back on that day, I had just returned from lunch and something felt off. I tried to dismiss the growing feeling of restlessness, not really knowing why I should be feeling this way. I just knew my intuition was telling me something wasn't right, and the feeling of uncertainty began to make itself known. My phone rang. I looked over at the caller ID and saw my boss calling me from his office. I picked up the receiver and greeted him. "Hey Chris."

"Will you come and see me please?" he asked me in a firm, yet empathetic voice.

"Sure," I said. "I'm on my way." I placed the receiver back on the cradle and closed my eyes. I stood up, pushing my chair back from my desk and turned to walk out of my office. My mind was racing. *Why does he always do that?* I asked myself.

Chris had this way of making me feel nervous whenever he called me or my co-workers about anything. And it wasn't intentional. In fact, I'll bet if he knew he scared the bejesus out of me when he summoned us to his office, he would likely laugh. You would never hear him say to one of us in a nonchalant manner, "Hey, can you come see me when you get a moment?" or "Stop by my office the next time you head to the copier." Not Chris. He always got straight to the point. It was very effective, because it worked like a charm each time. If you have ever had a supervisor, business partner, or friend that elicits this type of response, you know all too well how your mind can start jumping to conclusions about what it is they want to see you about.

As I walked down the hallway toward his office, my anxiety was beginning to build with each step. You know that type of anxiety when your breathing becomes shallower and heart starts to beat so fast, like it's going to come right out of your chest? It's that fight or flight mode feeling. That was the anxiety I was experiencing, and it was gaining momentum fast.

Three weeks prior, early rumors were circulating around the office regarding layoffs, office closures, staffing reductions, downsizing, and organizational restructure. Whatever term you label it, in the public sector, it is commonly referred to as a "reduction in force" (RIF).

I had conversations with my peers and even my boss following the early chatter and asked if I should be concerned. I was told it probably wasn't necessary as I was one of the highest senior managers in my unit and if staffing was on the line, it likely would be rescinded as our agency typically experiences further changes last minute. Still, I had this lingering doubt in the back of my mind that something didn't feel quite right, but I quietly pushed it aside and went about my business and brainstormed with my co-manager how would we handle the restructure if we lost a manager, not thinking that person would be me. I wasn't taking the planning all that seriously, and neither was anyone else.

I entered Chris' office and noticed a small stack of letters on his desk in front of him. He turned to me and had a look on his face like I have never seen before, one of despair and concern. He said to me quietly, "have a seat." I closed the door behind me and sat down slowly in the chair across from him. All he could say to me was, "I just received this," and pushed the letter in front of me to read. He looked away and out his window as I started to read.

"Dear Kimberly, This shall serve as your official notification that your position has been abolished..."

That was as far as I got before the tears filled my eyes. I wanted to throw up. I felt as though someone had just punched me in the stomach and my breath cut short. Oh my God, no! This isn't true. What am I going to do? Nothing had prepared me for that moment. I sat there numb, reading it, yet not believing it, it couldn't be true. It was a huge mistake, and someone clearly messed up. I had more years in my position than some of the others in my unit, so why me? This didn't make sense.

"Kim, from what I have been told, Civil Service Commission doesn't look at your years of service spent in management" he explained, his eyes sad. "Your total number of service years in the department is the basis for the involuntary bump. Because your co-worker has more seniority and because you both hold the same position and classification, they look at who is the less senior and abolish the least senior position."

"That's not fair," I whispered. I had worked so hard in my career with dedicating myself in returning to college to pursue my bachelor's degree, invited in opportunity after opportunity to learn, expand my knowledge, deepening my connection with my career, and earning that promotion to management to lead, mentor, learn and train. I looked forward to the next opportunity, the next challenge, in fact, I went so far as taking on small projects and used these as preparation tools in job interviews. Even though I wasn't offered the administrative and mid-management positions I interviewed for, I still viewed these as valuable experiences and leaned on these for personal and professional growth. And, as I sat in my boss's office that cold January day, I realized, that my forward momentum had been suddenly shifted into reverse. I would be returning to the caseworker position that I held seven years before.

It was all I could do in that moment to offer some words of my own courage to break the shock, disappointment, and sadness felt in the room. The only response I could speak was, "At least I still have a job and I'm not being been laid off" as I attempted to smile with some form of class as accepting this really shitty situation. The truth was I didn't want to accept it. This was *my* job, *my* hard work, why the hell *should* I be happy? I was being forced into a situation that I didn't want nor ask for.

I kept looking down at the letter staring at it, hoping each time I looked down, something different would be on the page. I was scared. At one point, I even thought this might be karma coming back to bite me for leaving my husband and wanting to end my marriage. So many emotions, so many feelings of despair, defeat, vulnerability began to emerge. My next biggest question was how in the hell would I financially afford this huge pay cut. I was separated from my husband, with a pending divorce which was scheduled for the week after my demotion was to take effect. Nothing like adding insult to injury. *Just wonderful*, I thought. *A demotion, a divorce, what else you got for me Universe? What other major life changing event do you have lined up for me? Things happen in threes, right?*

Chris instructed me to head home for the rest of the day. It was Friday afternoon and he knew me well enough to know that I wouldn't be able to concentrate on anything else. As I stood up and pushed the chair in, he stood up too, walked around his desk, gave me a strong hug and said me, "I'm so sorry Kim, we will get through this kiddo." I nodded and thanked him then walked out of his office, feeling deep hurt and pain not only for myself, but also for him.

In the weeks that followed my "involuntary demotion," I found myself searching the internet and spent hours looking for some guidance, relief, or advice from someone that had survived a demotion, layoff, downsizing, reduction in force, budget cuts. I came up with nothing that I could identify with. Had no one really been through a situation such as this? The endless news headlines of corporate America downsizing, outsourcing, getting rid of their brick and mortar locations, layoffs, demotions, reassignments, restructures, had no one really published a book about their experience that I could relate to? People get laid-off all the time, employees have set-backs every day across the country. The was nothing out there for me?

I searched relentlessly through online booksellers to find some miracle answer to my dilemma, some type of self-help book that talked straight to me and in some sense, desperately wanting to read something that would tell me what I wanted to hear that things would all work out. Nothing about this specific circumstance was seeking me out. I found books that provided legal help after being wrongfully demoted or how to bounce back at work after punitive action, or making the biggest mistake of your career, but that wasn't me. I needed help and help wasn't there. So, I decided if I needed help, the only person that could help me was myself because I certainly didn't create this situation...*or maybe I did?*

When you experience news such as this, it never really leaves you. It's one of those moments that sets a timeline in your life for what came before and after. Just like graduation, a deployment, marriage, having children, etc. It's important to honor your feelings and be okay with whatever comes up for you. For some, it may be anger, hurt, fear, rejection, or overjoyed, happiness, or relief. Whatever comes up for you, give yourself time and permission to process what has just happened. For a period of time following my demotion, I felt all alone, isolated. Like an outcast. I felt that nobody knew how I was feeling on the inside. It was as though everyone around me had returned to normalcy following the RIF and went on with their lives and here I was feeling anything but normalcy. It was as though nothing ever happened.

I felt so exposed and vulnerable as I sat in an open cubicle surrounded by my former staff, now turned peers. No one knew what to say to me. No one made eye contact with me. My peers lightly treaded lightly around me. The sidebar conversations in the hallways were filled with laughter, like nothing ever happened. Listening to the laughter made my skin crawl. I selfishly wanted everyone to feel just as bad as I did. At times, I could sense I was the topic of discussion with my peers because once I appeared around the corner out of nowhere, it would be obvious from their actions when looking at me that they ended their conversation rather abrupt and dispersed from the area. They weren't quite sure if they could trust me because I had been their supervisor. My former peers, now my managers, were also puzzled how to approach me or what they should or shouldn't say. They also weren't sure if they could trust me with confidential information because I was now a direct report. It sucked all the way around.

I had years of knowledge and expertise in certain areas and had been a sounding board for members of my management team, I contributed creative ideas, helped develop potential solutions, and now found myself sitting in a position where a fraction of my skills and abilities were being utilized. The same decisions I made just weeks before, I now need to consult with a manager on. The same two managers I helped train. How incredibly disheartening.

I remember sitting in my cubicle one afternoon and I overheard one of my former staff talking with a client about a complex situation. I knew exactly what she needed to do based on a local office policy I wrote and implemented. I could hear her talking with her client and then she hung up, and said to another co-worker, "I need to go talk this one over with a manager because it's above me on what I need to do." As she walked past my cubicle, I started to turn around in my swivel chair thinking that she would stop and ask me. Instead she walked right past, not even glancing my way or even acknowledge that I may know what she needed. I wasn't allowed to guide her and support her because it needed to come from a manager. *Are you freaking kidding me? My damn title received the demotion, not my brain.* It was like rubbing salt in a wound. It not only hurt deeply, it was insulting.

In addition to enduring the feelings of incompetency, the other side of this was shifting from a management mindset into an employee mindset. There is a difference. As an employee, there is a mindset that has a tendency to be more centered around individual needs and the work that is being performed. Typically speaking, when you are an employee, you usually don't concern yourself with your co-worker's performance problems, time and attendance issues, or if they fall behind in their work because they are more interested in their social media than the last spreadsheet that was sent. That's on them, not you. Your performance review is based on the work you perform, not your co-workers. This is not all-inclusive as I realize that there are distinct differences in team-based approaches in the private sector.

In management, however, you look at the whole picture, what is of the greatest good of the group of employees as a whole when making critical decisions. So now the employee who has performance problems, time and attendance issues, and is falling behind because they are doing the social media scroll is now your primarily responsibility along with your top performer who just informs you she will be out for 4-6 weeks for a medical procedure. All of this is your responsibility to figure out because your performance review is based on how everyone under you accomplishes the work. It's a "me becomes we" mindset from employee to manager. It is a complete mindset shift going from being concerned about those who work for you to only being concerned about yourself.

After some time had passed and once I consumed Mindy's Joyce Meyer devotional book in one afternoon, I slowly began to shift from a mindset of feeling inadequate to accountability. I began to take ownership of my feelings and sense of victimization. I started to receive some divine downloads from Spirit that perhaps I did play a role in causing my demotion. I started to feel a sense of responsibility in this situation that I wasn't ready to acknowledge or admit to myself up until that point. The prior three years leading up to my bump, I started to feel disengaged from my work. I was feeling stuck, not being challenged, and felt as though any growth or opportunities were at a standstill and nothing had any forward momentum. I felt detached from my purpose and stressed from a state of boredom and restraint.

I was becoming resentful with the lack of opportunities for creativity that were nonexistence. Although I attempted to be creative in my work and was able to introduce a few new concepts and small projects for staff, those fulfillments only lasted a short while before that feeling of monotony crept in again. Rather than refocusing on what I could do, I harbored feelings of insufficiency, which led to lack of motivation, and in some ways, being truly unhappy. My ego had quietly taken over and began inflicting sabotage. I spent those few years unconsciously creating destructive patterns of inner judgment, negative thoughts, and fearful beliefs that manifested themselves into a full blown inner-war.

The ego is the part of our personality that loves nothing more than creating undesirable experiences. The ego feeds off of fear, suspicion and hurt. The more we remain attached to our ego thoughts, the more we move further away from our authenticity. Our egos tend to want to take us out and have us remain in our comfort zones, because it's safe, while miserable at best. This is why many of us stay stuck in a place where we have movement but no motion. Our egos convince us just enough to make us believe we are doing something productive when in reality, we aren't doing anything, which leads to not feeling motivated and taking up residence in the 'comfortably numb' zone.

When we can relinquish our need to control outcomes and circumstances that bind us from seeing a bigger picture, it is then that we can allow ourselves to surrender. It is hard not knowing what's going to happen from one moment to the next, but we must trust that there is a loving force greater than us. This force is guiding us and supporting us even when it feels like are all alone in this process.

The steps below are the steps I took to be able to fully allow myself to surrender to a plan far greater than my own and get out of my own way.

STEP ONE: ACCEPTANCE

Acceptance does not mean that you agree with, condone, appreciate, or even like what has happened. Acceptance means that you know, regardless of what happened, that there is something bigger than you at work. It also means you know that you are okay and that you will continue to be okay.

- Iyanla Vanzant

First, accept the situation for what it was. Although nothing about it made sense, I had to seek acceptance in order for my healing to begin. I could have continued to dwell in my own misery, but I didn't want to be there. Holding on to something that is no longer serving you will just keep negative feelings alive, holds you captive to your pain and lowers your energy. The moment you decide and let your negative feelings fall away, and accept what is, you are on the road to freedom. When you let go of who you think you are supposed to be, the Universe can swoop in and help you become who you are really meant to be.

Surrender is not giving up or saying that everything is perfectly okay; it's actually just the opposite. It is the willingness to give up, but not in the way we think giving up may mean. We don't give in to the situation, we give in to the idea that we should be managing the situation instead of trying to control the outcome. It is exhausting to try to be in charge all the time, which is why acceptance is so vital to your inner peace. Surrender is recognizing and accepting what you can't change. We do this by releasing expectations and allowing what will be to be. Keep in mind….this is a process, certainly not an overnight fix. Surrender is a practice that you must choose to do each day, so that it becomes easier and easier and becomes a natural thing you do.

We have a human tendency to control our life because we think if we don't, what will happen. Control is the result of being attached to a specific outcome—one we are certain is the best for us. When we try to control a situation we are trying to play God. When we are attached to the outcome, the universe cannot come in and help give us what we really need, which may be better than what we think and believe. The energy behind surrender accomplishes so much more than the desperate energy of control.

Think about the difference between the two: Control energy is tight, restricted, and often manic. Your mind may shift from the past to the future very quickly as you try to figure out the solution. Now switch to surrender mode; you are calm, peaceful, and connected to your truest self.

You are more present in the moment and you can see there are things happening behind the scenes to help support your desires and needs. Trust that. Lean into that. I guarantee you will be supported. You let go of the attachment by being present in this moment. Surrendering is the free falling backwards into the unknown and trusting that spirit will catch you, and this must be done from a place of trust. You have to give it all you got and completely surrender to the Universe's plan.

STEP TWO: TRUST

The second step was trusting that this situation was brought to me for a specific reason and, I would be brought through it with Spirit at my side. While I was scared and afraid of what I was leaving behind, because it was all I had known and become comfortable with, I trusted that what was being taken from me was going to be replaced by something much bigger and better that would lead me down a new path opening new doors of opportunities and meeting new people along the way that would eventually lead me to where I was meant to go. Trust isn't an easy thing to do.

We doubt whether spirit will intervene on our behalf guiding us, supporting us in all ways. We often wonder if miracles will truly unfold because we lack faith in the promises that He has made for us, mostly because we tend to believe that the bad things that has happened to us could have been prevented. Trust is like a muscle. It is necessary to exercise and practice it so that it can become stronger. When you begin to realize that there is an energy presence of love that is available to you any time, your perspective on your situation will begin to shift and what you will witness is miracles beginning to develop. Once you stop relying on your own strength and relying on a presence far greater than your own, that's where spirit intervenes and will lift you to new heights.

It was intimidating returning to a position that had changed throughout the years, but I trusted that God wasn't done with me yet, and this certainly wasn't my final destination. I placed my complete trust in Him and declared many times, "I don't know why I am going through this or why this is happening to me, but I trust it, I trust You. I trust that You are on my side and won't let me fail. I trust that everything I need will be provided to me and my family and that the right people and circumstances will cross my path to help guide me, support me, and offer their grace and love." Your thoughts are very powerful and are a reflection of you. They can affect your mood, your attitude, and actions. Replacing your negative thoughts with positive thoughts can elevate your energy and create a place for peace within your heart that allows trust to be developed with ease. Before my demotion went into effect, one of my staff left a rock on my desk with a note of hope on it. The rock was inscribed:

"Trust in the Lord with all your heart. And lean not on your own understanding; in all ways acknowledge Him, And He shall direct your paths."

- Proverbs 3:5-6

Her note explained that she was given this rock during a difficult time and looked at it many times providing her with comfort and hope and to always trust that while we may not understand it, it is being used for our highest and greatest good. I still have the rock and her note which is kept in my small dresser along with other small items that have been gifted to me in times of trial. Once I completely turned my trust over, the miracles began to unfold. Expect good things to happen. Expect that spirit will do for you what you cannot do for yourself. This certainly does not mean it will be easy but will require you to do your part. Find peace that the universe is always conspiring to work miracles on your behalf. All you have to do it trust that they will.

STEP THREE: PRAY

Each day following my receipt of my letter, I intentionally made it part of my daily routine to pray. I carved out time and space at the start of my day, several times during the day, and at the end of my day to have the most important conversation I could have. Sharing with God my fears, my hopes, my needs, but also thanking him for leading me towards the highest and greatest good. Thanking Him for helping me inch closer toward realizing why this was happening and understanding the good that could come from this devastation. I prayed often. I prayed in the car on the way to work, I prayed in the shower in the morning, I prayed at Walmart standing in line-those prayers were a little different, I asked for patience! Each time I prayed I felt the love of Spirit rush though me knowing my thoughts and feelings were being heard with divine love and grace, I felt my mind, body, and spirit soften knowing that I was heard and that I would be taken care of.

Every morning, on my way to work, I would pray the same prayer over and over:

"Dear God, I don't understand why this is happening to me, but that's okay, because I trust it. I trust You. I know deep within my heart that you didn't get me this far in my career, just to get me this far. I know you have taken me off a path and are ready to show me another that will serve a much greater audience. Thank you for loving me and being with me. I know you are with me. Amen."

Each time I recited that prayer, I instantly felt my anxiety lift and a sense of peace settle in to that space. The more I said it, the more I connected to it. It became my mantra to declare, "I didn't come this far to only come this far!" I would often ask for guidance or direction of what it was that I was supposed to do. I felt lost and scattered. I came into work and felt like a housefly coming out of its winter hibernation, that awkwardly flies around with not much speed and certainly no sense of direction. I lost my bearings and experienced difficulty processing simple duties not knowing what simple task to perform, or how to look busy in a position that I no longer understood how to do. I wasn't able to process much. It was mentally and emotional taxing on me. So, I turned to prayer, the one thing at the time that offered relief and clarity.

Around the time I increased my prayer conversations, I also began listening to Joyce Meyer. My co-worker had lent me her collection of CDs to listen to on my commute to and from work. I willingly took them and started to listen to her messages of hope. One of Joyce's sermons that I listened to was the manner in which we pray. I immediately turned all my attention to her and learn that if there was a way I could improve my conversations, I was ready to try it. I found it helpful to listen as Joyce explained that when we pray with an impatient mentality, such as saying, "Please, God, Please," grant me this or grant me that, we are actually placing a desperate energy into our conversations. This totally made sense and I noticed that I started shifting from desperate state of "begging" to intentionally praying.

STEP FOUR: ALLOW

> *"You surrender to a lot of things which are not worthy of you. Surrender instead to your radiance, your integrity, your beautiful human grace."*

\- Yogi Bhajan

Once we pray, the next step is to get out of our own way and allow God to do what His will is, not ours. While I held firm belief that my outcome would be what my heart desired, I still allowed Him to lead the way. Oftentimes, when we pray, we ask God for what it is we think we need. When we pray for what is of the highest and greatest good for all, we get out of the way and allow God to bring forth the best possible outcome. By allowing God to intervene and trust Him to bring us through our storm, He will in turn crown your efforts with success.

Allowing is simply releasing resistance. Another side of allowing is trusting, which is woven in step two above. Being patient and having faith that the desires of your heart will manifest and will show up in your life as they are meant to. However, it's up to you and your ability to allow things to happen and emerge without having to manipulate or control other people or situations to make them happen. Those of us who tend to have a controlling nature and like to be in charge may find this to be a work in progress. It certainly isn't easy, but with some patience and practice, it can flourish. Allowing doesn't mean that you just give up, it means that we love ourselves enough to give up the attachment to what is allowing anxiety and resistance to limit new opportunities.

Letting go means releasing yourself from something that no longer serves your purpose. It also means removing unhelpful situations and belief systems from your life so that you can create space room for more meaningful experiences that are conducive to positive wellbeing and happiness.

When we surrender and wave the white flag, we are allowing ourselves the grace and compassion to give ourselves the time and the energy to face the next obstacle. Often, we become so attached to how we believe an outcome should be that we forget that there are always other ways to navigate life.

When we can begin to shift our awareness to these principles, we begin to heal the rejection we experienced and can begin focusing our energy on doing something different in the healthier manner to move forward.

Recognize and Reflect:

1. Describe one or two situations, personal or professional, that have recently occurred in which you felt stressed.

2. As you journal your responses, begin to take note if it was the situation itself or perhaps your reaction that caused the stressful situation. Reflect on this question as you respond to the following question. Was this situation worth getting upset about, or if there was another way to respond differently?

3. What can you do to lean into surrender?

The reason many people in our society are miserable, sick, and highly stressed is because of an unhealthy attachment to things they have no control over.

- Steve Maraboli

Wherever you are, be all there.

- Jim Elliot

Chapter Two

HAPPINESS IS AN INSIDE JOB

A few years prior to my demotion, I could begin to feel myself slip into a state of burnout. When we think of burnout, we tend to view this as a state of chronic stress that can often lead to feelings of mental and emotional depletion, resentment and detachment from things once found enjoyable, feelings of ineffectiveness, and lack of accomplishment. However, burnout can also be recognized as a mismatch between a person's subconscious needs and demands of work or personal responsibilities.

Imagine a nurse who prefers limited patient exposure, charting patient progress, but has the role of primary patient care. Or a social worker that excels at building partnerships and establishing social connections, yet is inundated with spreadsheets, reviewing statistics and data. Are your job expectations and subconscious needs in alignment with one another? If they are, your needs are being met. However, if employees are not performing in these identified roles, burnout can surface.

Corporations and organizations actually do more harm than good to their employees by hiring them into roles and responsibilities that aren't in alignment with their needs, desires, talents, and strengths. If companies do not routinely check in with one of their most valuable assets, their employees, the chances of disconnect and discontent can increase, leaving employees to experience burnout sooner. When companies recognize the gifts their employees already have and tap into that by allowing them to thrive and grow, success will naturally follow.

We are always evolving and changing throughout life, changing direction, finding new interests, seeking new passions, and figuring out easier methods of solving challenges. We are anything but linear beings. When we are no longer in alignment with the work we perform, or the service we provide to others, that is when we are more susceptible to emotional and mental burnout. That is what slowly started to happen to me, although I didn't recognize it at the time. I felt myself become disengaged from my work because my subconscious needs were not being met. The unhappiness surrounding my work started to mirror what was also happening in my personal life around this same time frame. What appeared on the outside, was that I had my shit together and life was really great for me. I had an amazing career, a spouse that also had also just landed his professional career, a spacious home, and two beautiful children.

On the inside, revealed a much different story that I dismissed for years as unhappiness for a lack of self-love, and self-worth. I was disconnected from me. I was the woman who sacrificed her own needs to make sure everyone around her was the priority, making sure those around me were taken care of, being all things, to everyone, at all times. I became exhausted and started to become resentful, which was a feeling I wasn't comfortable with. That's not who I am, and it bothered me that I felt so unhappy. My subconscious needs were not being met and I was the only one that stood in the way of meeting them.

I took up running as an escape from the void I was feeling in between the bouts of happiness. Little did I know that this escape would lend itself to teaching me valuable lessons and revealed something that was buried inside. The internal changes and shifts I grew through also uncovered things about me that I didn't realize I was capable of doing. Running happened by sheer accident. I wasn't planning on becoming a runner. I wasn't looking for a new hobby or outlet to expend my unhappiness, but, sometimes we don't seek these things out, they seek us out and find us instead. I would hardly consider myself an athlete in any form. I didn't play sports in high school because I was self-conscious of my lack of athletic ability and whether I could maintain more than 30 minutes of physical activity at a time. Those were limiting beliefs that I eventually busted right through like no one's business when I crossed the finish line after completing my first marathon three years later. I found running, or maybe I should say, running found me. I was out of shape and miserable with my weight after I had our second baby. I felt flabby, gross, and unhealthy and while I wanted to lose weight and get in shape, the idea of doing anything cardio vascular was not in my plan. The Universe had other ideas for me.

We had an unusual early Spring in 2011 and had been spending some time outdoors soaking in the warmth of the sun, breathing in the scent of fresh earth that had been covered with a blanket of snow, watching the last of the icicles melt, dripping from the roof. My 6-year-old wanted to take his new bike for a ride, so I walked beside him as he pedaled along with his training wheels tipping from side to side gently touching the ground. We made our way across the highway and onto another roadway that wasn't as busy, and had a nice big hill that kids loved to ride their bikes down. As we made our way over the crest of the hilltop, the downward slope of the hill began to invite my sons bike along for the ride. He stopped pedaling and began giggling as he felt the hill take over and enjoyed the momentum he was gaining.

I looked farther ahead and could see a car barreling fast toward us and I panicked. I called out for my son to slow down and stop, but he couldn't hear me because the wind was whipping by his ears as he gained faster momentum. I broke into a run sprinting and calling out for him to stop. He turned around and looked back at me and saw me 'chasing him', which he thought was funny as he let out a can't-catch-me giggle. I was in full Forrest Gump mode as I bolted my way arms pumping in the air, as that would get me to him faster. I finally caught up to him as the car turned into a driveway before making its way to us. My son stopped pedaling and stopped his bike. He was giggling. I was profusely sweating, I wanted to puke, my lungs were on fire, my feet were throbbing. *And people do this for fun?* I thought to myself. *Screw this.*

The next morning, I crawled out of bed and felt as though every muscle I never knew existed were kindly introducing themselves to me by making sure they each got my attention. I limped my way to the bathroom and looked at myself in the mirror and thought, what the hell is going on with me? I stood there for a moment and looked over at my sweaty clothes I had left there from the night before and realized my soreness was from my short sprint chasing my kid. I didn't exactly like how sore I felt, but I also knew if that I was going to make any changes to lose weight and get healthy, I may have to hurt and get uncomfortable before it stops hurting and becomes comfortable.

Over the next few days, I returned to the same road and repeated my sprint run down the hill and walked back up. After a couple of weeks, I could feel myself going longer distances without having to stop and walk so often. The bursts of short sprints slowly turned into a slower pace of turning out a couple hundred yards, a half-mile, then a mile. I was doing it. I was running. I started to feel a connection to something yet couldn't necessarily extract what that something was. I liked the feeling and the endorphins that running released for me. Interesting coming from the person who never wanted to break a sweat or do anything physical. Running also offered me an outlet from stress and frustrations I was feeling. It was a way for me to discharge negative energy in a productive manner rather than coming home and crabbing to my family about what kind of a crappy day I had or vent about a disgruntled client or co-worker. It allowed me to head outdoors into the fresh air, breathe heavily, stir up inner emotions to bring them to the surface, pound out the frustration, and leave it on the pavement to return refreshed to my family.

I was still uncertain of my newfound ability to run, as I still held onto that self-limiting belief that I never amounted to an athlete. My ego wanted to take me out planting doubt in my mind, but I pushed back. I wanted to figure out what that connection was that I couldn't quite identify. I participated in my first 5k race two months after I started running. I hadn't planned on running a 5k, much like I hadn't planned on becoming a runner, but somehow one of my staff convinced me that I should challenge myself.

Two weeks after I discovered my inner athlete who had been hiding inside of her repressed locker room, I still wasn't convinced that I was doing much of anything beyond what I did in high school trekking around the perimeter of a basketball court completing 12 laps and calling it a run. I had just finished reviewing some case files at work and wanted to return them to one of my staff before she left for the day. I picked up the large stack from my desk and made my way to the middle hallway toward her cubicle. When I turned the corner, there was a small gathering outside her cubicle as I walked in on the conversation she and a few of my other staff were engaged in. It sounded like they were scheming something as playful laughter erupted from their conversation.

One of my staff looked up at me approaching her with her stack of files and greeted me with a big smile as she paused her conversation with her peers.

"Hey Kim!"

"Hi there Leann, what are you all scheming about over here?" I asked curiously as I smiled back at her and my other staff and placed the files on her desk.

"We were just convincing one another to get a group together here at work to run a 5k race that the hospice house is hosting as their fundraiser," she explained.

"Really?" I asked. *"So, mind if I ask how many miles that is? I'm sorta new to this whole new running thing and I'm not sure what a 5K is."* I went on to share with her that I somewhat stumbled into running, with a whole lot of walking, two weeks prior.

"A 5k is 3.1 miles," Leann explained. *"Why don't you join us?"* she asked.

I let out a laugh and said, *"Oh goodness, there is NO way I could run 3.1 miles. I am barely up to running a half of a mile without stopping. When is this race anyway?"*

"It's in 6 weeks," she said. *"You have plenty of time to train."*

"Train?! 6 weeks to build up enough endurance to run 3.1 miles? It might as well be 300 miles," I exclaimed. *"There is no way I can run that whole distance!"*

"You don't have to run the entire race, silly girl. Just go at your own pace and do your best. There is no rule that you have to run all 3.1 miles nonstop. C'mon, just try it," she said trying her best to now convince me too. Now I know why the others were laughing.

Before I could politely decline, she reached for a manila folder on her desk and pulled out a sheet of paper from it. *"Here you go,"* she said. *"I have extra registration forms and this one has your name on it."* I stood there for a minute holding onto the registration form in my hand, like a baton in a relay race. I didn't want to drop it, but I wasn't entirely convinced to run with it either. She reached over to a cup on her desk that held her pens and took one out that already had the cap removed, and said, *"Here's a pen if you want to fill it out right now. I'll bet you will surprise yourself by what your body and mind can accomplish,"* she said. *"I have faith in you."*

And that was all it took. I sat down in the chair in her cubicle, picked up the pen and began filling it out. *"I cannot believe I am doing this,"* I said.

"I am SO proud of you!" she exclaimed with a big grin and clapped her hands. *"We are going to have so much fun!"*

"You bring the fun, and I'll bring my nerves," I said. And just like that, I signed up for my first 5k race. While it felt a little intimidating, it also had a nice blend of excitement with it. I hadn't just stepped outside of my comfort zone, I catapulted from it.

The day of the race arrived, and I showed up an hour and a half before the race even started. I had a nightmare the week prior that I was late to arrival and the race had already started. To avoid that possibility, I made sure I arrived to the start line early. I arrived so early that no one was there yet, and so then I questioned if I really was late or had the date wrong. *Gah!* I went back to my car to calm myself down and relax a bit. After a few minutes, I slowly saw people begin to filter in, which made me feel better. I saw one of my co-workers and then more of my co-workers began to show up. *"Thank God!"* I thought. My support crew is here. The race started an hour later, and I found myself no longer feeling anxious, I was challenging myself and letting my body show me how strong she was. It was an incredible feeling and I smiled each time someone ran past me.

After I came across the finish line, I was so happy and joyful, and most of all, I was so damn proud of myself for doing something I never thought I would push myself to do. After my natural endorphin release that I felt from crossing the finish line, I was hooked. I went on to run nine more races that summer. Following my last race of the season that year, after I crossed the finish line, I realized what that connection was that I had tried to figure out each time I laced up my shoes, strapped my phone onto my armband and turned up the music on my playlist.

The last race I ran was a 5.7 mile race. It was the longest distance I had ran and I was extremely nervous. I was a new runner and the thought of stopping to have to walk during a race was almost enough to have me back out. It was yet another way the ego tried to trick me into thinking I wasn't good enough and couldn't do it. Again, I pushed back and wanted to forge ahead. The race started, and I had hundreds of other runners that surrounded me.

Because I was a new runner, I hadn't trained my energy to start out slow and steady. I typically was so geeked up when I started a race, that I would start to lose my steam right around mile 2. For a 5k race, which is 3.1 miles, that was fine, because the last mile, I knew I knew I was over the halfway mark, and that was enough to keep me going. This race though was 5.7 miles. I wanted to show myself that I could run the entire race without having to stop and walk, so I mentally told myself, I would have to start out slow. At mile two, I could feel my ego start to talk to me and slowly interrupt my pace and slow me down. I wasn't having any of it. I didn't want to stop, I couldn't stop. I was committed to putting in the hard work and coming out on top showing myself I would not let a new challenge take me out. When I made it past the 5k mark, I smiled and gave myself a little inward pep talk telling myself good job! I continued and pushed myself forward feeling the challenge the new distance was offering. As I made my way to the final leg of the race, I could sense an emotion growing inside. It was that same feeling I had experienced and connected to, and I felt it growing with each step I took toward the finish chute.

My sister was waiting for me at the finish line with her camera ready to snap some pictures of me. I came around the corner and saw the big banner sign that read: FINISH, I felt this lump rise in my throat. I kept going feeling this rising sensation that was about to bust though the surface. As I ran through the chute, I looked up at the massive digital clock that let runners know what their finish time was. I saw: 1:01:01. I stepped across the finish line, with my arms raised high above my head and smiled so big! The race volunteer handed me my finisher's medal and I felt this wave of emotion, the one that I was connected to and finally revealed itself to me that afternoon: *Achievement*. I felt tears begin to well up and a sheer wave of pride wrapped around me as I allowed the tears of joy and happiness roll down my cheeks. That was the connection. It wasn't just the achievement of running a distance, it was celebrations of many accomplishments that running offered.

It gave me strength and endurance, both physically and mentally, I felt more energetic and alert, I pushed myself past my own comfort zone, but most of all, running introduced me to surrendering to a plan that had been already laid out for me. I just needed to be willing to let go of my own insecurities about not being an athlete, drop the limiting belief that I would never or could never, and trust that what I was experiencing was all part of a plan that was taking me on a new path of charting the direction of where I was headed. Becoming a runner laid a foundation for me to handle adversities that came my way. It also opened doors to new friendships being made, and a chance for friendships I had with old friends to be revitalized. The Universe just knows who, what, and when you need someone or something to be placed in your path.

Three months prior to my demotion, I became a Reiki Master. I learned about reiki healing through one of my running buddies and became so intrigued after I experienced a session that I found myself becoming drawn to this healing modality. I suppose in some sense, I didn't find reiki, reiki found me. Reiki was another way that I learned about what was happening to me inside that was the cause for feeling unsettled and unhappy. Through reiki, I discovered new ways of shifting my energy from a place of ego and fear to love and patience. This was exciting for me to learn how to apply these principles as I am generally not a patient person. If you are like me, I sometimes have the tendency to want to rush things or become frustrated when things don't happen as quickly as I think they should. That's the ego side of us. The loving side is to lean into patience and trust that all that is meant for you will fall together perfectly and in exact alignment, just as it is supposed to.

During my reiki training, I learned of something called a vision board, which is a board that has a collection of pictures that represent whatever you want to be, want to do, or have in your life. A vision board serves as a visual tool to help get you clear and focus on specific life goals you want to bring forth, even if you don't know how you will achieve them. The intent behind the vision board is that the how these will come to fruition will be figured out for you. If your feelings are in complete alignment with that which you are desiring, it will manifest itself into form.

On a Sunday afternoon, I thought to myself, *why not make one and see what happens?* It was like putting together a giant scrapbook collage on one piece of poster board. I decorated it with pictures and stickers. I placed images of a camping trip I wanted to take, a new digital camera, a house, along with a few other places I wanted to travel to and things I would like to have. After I created it, I noticed I had some open space on the board, which I thought I would leave open just in case something else came to mind that I could add later.

Two weeks after tacking my vision board to the wall in my bedroom, I thought of that other thing I wanted for vision board. Since I had been unhappy and in a frame or burnout at work, I figured, why not put something on there that represents what I would like to happen. When I arrived home that evening from work, I dug out my cube of sticky notes and handwrote a goal on one of the pieces that simply stated, *New opportunities at work.* I slapped it on my vision board in the empty space and said, "There, show me what you got." I didn't really know who or what entity I was talking to at that point as I was relatively new to reiki and how our thoughts create what will become reality. For all I knew, nothing would happen other than I had this large poster in my room with pictures and stickers on it that looked like it belonged in my bedroom when I was 12.

I had no idea that what I intentionally wrote out and stuck on a board that I would look at every morning would come back and bite me straight in the ass three months later when that *New opportunity at work,* manifested itself right into form and landed me flat on my face. *There, take that Kim. You wanted a new opportunity? You got one.* (A word of caution, be careful what you ask for, vision boards do work.) Because I hadn't specifically stated what new opportunities at work I had intended, I more or less just assumed that my thoughts would be good opportunities at work. However, what I was feeling at work, wasn't empowering, wasn't positive, wasn't from a state of happiness, joy, or excitement. I was essentially throwing out some random statement in hopes it would boomerang back and get me on track. However, what I was feeling and what I wanted was in complete misalignment with one another and proved itself by giving me exactly what I asked for, a new opportunity at work. An opportunity to return to a position I held 7 years prior. What I was seeking was a launch, a catapult, something to propel me into something greater and more fulfilling. What I got was the complete opposite.

I used to think my happiness would be filled when I got the promotion at work, or when my side photography business took off, or when we paid off our credit cards, or when we got the new vehicle, and finally took that trip as a family that I had desperately asked for. While these things initially brought me great happiness and joy, it was only short term before the excitement wore off and I found myself seeking the next new thing to fill that happiness gap. My ex-husband would say to me, nothing is ever enough for you. He was absolutely right. Nothing filled me up and nothing has lasting fulfillment. External sources can be a contributor to our inner joy, not the lone influence in fulfillment of such happiness.

If what we are feeling, thinking, and believing is unhappiness, boredom, burnout, or fatigue, and project that energy into important areas of our life, such as our marriages or career, then we are going to attract more of the same. When you can recognize what you don't want, that's good. This is when we begin to notice and become aware of the difference and in turn, begin to shift the way we want to feel, think, and believe that something more is available to us.

We just have to become willing to shift into that frequency. It takes time and intentional practice. This is not a one-time decision by declaring that today and for the rest of my life I decide to feel, think, and believe something good is coming my way. It's an intentional decision that we must choose to make each day. Of course we all have weak moments that try to take us out mentally and spiritually, that's what makes us human. However, when we can notice and become aware of them, is when we can begin to shift into a different, more loving, compassionate mindset toward ourselves and others. Over time I slowly began to figure out what I had been doing and more so, feeling, that created this situation. Once I understood that happiness is an inside job, I began to lean into that and experienced breakthrough after breakthrough along the way.

Recognize and Reflect:

1. In what ways are you aligned with the work you perform?

2. Describe a time in which you experienced burnout or disconnect from an important area of your life.

3. List three steps you can take to lean into your inner joy and happiness.

It's not what happens to you,
but how you react to it that matters.

- Epictetus

Chapter Three

EVERYDAY IS AN INTERVIEW

When I left the office the afternoon after receiving the news of my fate, I picked up my cell phone on my way home and started to dial the first person I had leaned on for the last 14 years. As the phone started to ring, I heard his voice on the other end. "Hello?" he asked quickly. My eyes filled with tears, my voice trembling, "Jay. . . .it happened. I got my letter. I'm scared. I don't know what I'm going to do..." as my need for a deep breath took over while waiting for his response.

I had told my soon to be ex-husband at Christmas that there were rumors of potential layoffs and downsizing, but that I really wasn't worried as I was the most senior manager, not to mention, the State had a reputation for threatening shut-downs and layoff's before, which always seem to be rescinded moments beforehand. I assured him, at the same time, trying to assure myself that I wouldn't be affected. I had shared this news with him just to give him a heads-up as our divorce was pending just a few weeks later. "We'll figure it out Kimmy," he went on to tell me. "It'll be okay, you are a smart girl, things will be fine." I pushed aside the tears and said, thank you. I then hung up and called my dad. At 39 years old, I suppose one is never too old to call their parents when they are in crisis and need help.

My dad was at work when he got my call. I shared with him a similar account of what I shared with my spouse, yet this time, I felt much more composed. He told me he would meet me at my apartment. When he entered my doorway, I was sitting at the kitchen table staring at my letter. He had a look of care and concern as he saw my face still stained from the tears. He came over to where I was sitting, gave me a hug and he took a seat just across the table from me. I pushed my letter in front of him to read, just like my boss did to me an hour before. He started to read it, studied it for a moment, took off his glasses and placed it on the table before looking up at me.

I knew what was coming. My dad is one of those guys who tends to analyze complex circumstances before jumping to a conclusion, carefully evaluating both sides before offering his thoughts on a situation. Just as I knew he would, he assumed his analytical take on the situation to offer me some comfort and perhaps insight from a managerial sense.

"This was a business decision, you know that right?" he asked me.

"Of course, dad, I know this" I replied.

"Hmm," he said again, and looked back down at the letter. Even my dad was speechless, and he isn't speechless very often. My dad has served our township as an elected official and has a reputation for his candor and his eloquent ability to speak up and when he does, most ears tune in to what he has to say. And it's exactly why I called him. I wanted to hear what he had to say about the situation, knowing that he may have a different perspective and I respected his take on the situation.

My dad also has been known to provide advice or his take on a situation from a business and professional standpoint instead of a loving father perspective at times. He tends to find teachable moments and doesn't waste an opportunity to educate someone on anything at any time. I remember once when I was in high school, our volleyball team was asked to host players from an out of town team in our homes overnight as we didn't have a hotel in our small town at the time. I was so excited to host two other girls from another school and invited one of my friends to join us. My dad picked us up that Friday evening after a welcome dinner for the other team and drove us to our house. On the drive home, my dad was being an awesome host and was engaging in light conversation with the girls we just met the hour before. It was in the middle of winter and later in the evening, so everything was dark and only illuminated by a couple of random street lights.

We turned onto the road leading to our house and my dad immediately entered his professional mode and began educating the girls in the backseat about the history of our area, how many islands we have, and why only two have bridges that lead to those islands. As we approached the first bridge, we slowed down as though they could see anything in the pitch black and explained that what we were driving over was considered the first 'causeway' to the islands. It was a good thing it was dark inside the car, as my face turned red and I could feel the girls and my friend in the backseat giggle at the professional speech they were receiving. I didn't have the heart to tell my dad that a bunch of 14-year-old girls really weren't interested in the history of ice fishing in our area.

I have learned over the years that when I elicit his advice or want to talk with him, I have to establish some "unwritten" ground rules for discussion and usually have to preface it with, *Dad, I need you to listen to me as your daughter right now, not as a business executive, not as a direct report, or a constituent. I don't need you to fix anything or do anything, or analyze it, I just need to be heard.* That usually helps both of us as he can relax and not engage his mind to begin fixing my woes, and it helps me as I can freely speak and not wonder if he's listening to me or formulating a tactical response in his mind. This time, however, I needed a nice blend of both my dad in his father role and his business side. He delivered just as I needed.

Over the next half hour, he listened to me as I tried to rationalize my situation desperately searching for solutions to prevent this from happening. I went back and forth many times between denial and acceptance. I was throwing out ideas like a bad cast and reeling them in as quickly as I tossed one idea out after the other.

"Maybe I should take a leave of absence, so I can sort some things out. I have almost three months of sick leave and two months of vacation. It would save me money by not driving to work and I could have time to process what is happening. Wait! No,

that would only delay the inevitable. I would still go back to a job that doesn't want me and I don't want it."

"There is a supervisor position that is vacant that is two hours from here. What if I applied for it and expanded my commute each day. Lots of people drive insane distances to go to work each day. No, that doesn't make much sense either for me as a single mom. The weather is unpredictable in the winter and I would be spending the difference in my pay with gas money. Maybe that's not a good idea…"

"Should I look for an entirely new job? Who the heck around here is hiring in January with pay comparable to what I was making before? No. That would mean giving up all the years I have spent here that contribute toward my retirement."

"Dad, don't you have any legislative buddies that you could call in a favor to and advocate for a reversal of this whole mess? That's a far stretch but I don't know what else to do."

I realized after I was rambling non-stop that he had stopped replying. I looked up at him staring back at me with a blank look. They were just negotiation tactics that I was having with my dad, who had no more say in the situation as I did. At the end of my venting, my situation was still the same. He got up from the table to leave. I know without a doubt his head was spinning as much as mine was at that point, although I wouldn't have known it. As I walked him out, I thanked him for coming over.

He said to me in the most supportive way, "More than anything Kimberly, keep your emotions under control. I know this is one is a tough one. You've worked very hard to get where you are at. It's not over honey. This isn't the end. Many eyes are going to be watching you and how you handle yourself." I nodded my head, I knew he was right and also knew that while I knew I would have hard moments throughout my days, I would need to pray for the strength to sturdy my feelings.

Keeping your emotions under control is easier said than done. If you are like me, we tend to wear our hearts on our sleeves and can barely master a poker face, let alone maintain one for very long. Usually getting too emotional isn't good. When we show too much of our feelings it's often viewed as unprofessional and can interrupt the calm environment that should be prevalent in most workplaces. If we can allow ourselves to have feelings and express them in a healthy manner when it is safe to do so, we will have a more positive and faster response to healing than if we were to mask them by concealing them deep down inside.

When we don't allow ourselves to properly process our emotions, we can actually do more long-term damage to our brains. You know the people who you see on your social media page that post #fuckfeelings after they just experienced a break up or tragedy that has hit them hard, or impacted them? How about the people you may know that constantly avoid dealing with emotions, and utter the words, "I'm fine" when asked how they are? You know they really aren't "fine." You know one or two of those individuals right? Or, maybe there is a chance that as you are reading this, you may be thinking, *she just described me.*

When we don't handle our negative feelings productively, we can oftentimes send ourselves into a mental state of despair, leading to secondary trauma. Clinical depression has been linked to a shortage of dopamine as well as two other neurotransmitters, serotonin and norepinephrine. Failure to process negative emotions can cut off our supply of these vital chemicals our brains require for proper functioning. Trying to suppress our emotions in professional settings isn't always the answer. Our feelings and emotions serve an important role in problem solving, inspiring others, along with other cognitive functions that we use at work. The question should be not about how to hide our feelings, but how to channel them into productive uses instead.

In the following weeks, I had started to pack my office and started to clean out old files, containing client complaints, old reports, employee evaluations, boss's day cards, and a box of brand new business cards that I just received. I begrudgingly thought to myself, well that's a waste of money, as I tossed them into the garbage. If this organization really cared about saving money and their employee's jobs, perhaps they should take a closer look at what useless shit they spend their money on. *Easy Kim, I thought, keep it together. You have every right to be upset, but don't do it here. Every day is an interview.*

"Every day is an interview," is a phrase my boss used quite often around the office. He also said, "Make sure you don't kick too much ass on the way up your career ladder because you never know whose ass you night have to kiss on the way back down." Duly noted and solid advice. What he meant by every day is an interview is that our daily actions are always being watched and observed by not only our peers, but leadership as well. If we have crappy attitudes or do just the bare minimum to get our jobs done every day, it is noticed, and if you don't think it is, think again. Our response to change, stress, disappointment, and failure are all being watched. It was priceless advice that I took to heart early in my management career and made sure that I was even more aware of my attitude and the manner in which I carried myself.

In time, I slowly began to notice others behavior and knew exactly what he meant by this. You may have witnessed this at times in your career too. What was most revealing to me was when a promotional opportunity was on the horizon, people would unexpectedly come out of hibernation from the cubicles to "volunteer" for special tasks or projects, or suddenly arrive early to work or stay past their end of their shift. Employees morphed into loving, kind, helpful beings. The attitudes were more cheerful and as the date of interviews drew closer, it was as though the office was on the verge of everyone holding hands around the copier singing kumbaya.

Once interviews were over and the candidate was announced, the behavior of those that were not offered the position flipped like a switch and went right back to conducting themselves in the same manner before any mention of a promotion. Some employees grumbled, gossiped, and groaned over the chosen candidate. One or two would downright have a chip on their shoulder. Certainly not the best way to be remembered or recognized should there be another opportunity for advancement down the road. "Every day is an interview" is exactly what it is. Your actions and behaviors are consistently being noticed and if you don't think they are, you may want to think again. Your response to a less than ideal situation will be observed and duly noted for the future. You don't have to like a situation, but don't demonstrate your ignorance. Have some self-respect and grace. This isn't about you or your ego.

At the same time I was bumped out of my position, several of my peers in other areas around the state were also being bumped from theirs. One of my peers, whom I had become close with over the years, was also affected by the reduction in force. Her response to the situation reflected the #fuckfeelings mentality.The week before Christmas, I was sitting in my office and received an instant chat request from her.

"Got a Minute?" she asked.

"Sure," I typed, *"give me a call."*

My phone rang immediately. "Hey Ann, what's up?" I asked

"So have you been put on notice?" she asked.

"What are you taking about?" I asked. "What notice?"

"This place is getting ready to lay people off and cause bumps across our department", she blurted with a sense of anxiety in her voice, "I just came from Mark's office (her boss) and he told me that I'm getting bumped out of my job. Real fuckin' nice, get this news right before Christmas."

"Wow....I am so sorry, I had no idea." All I had heard was rumors, but now, there appeared to be some truth to it. "Why did you ask if I was put on notice?" I asked her.

"Because they (our employer) are eliminating our classification," she replied.

It still didn't make sense to me. My boss had indicated that eliminating our classification could be the case, but nothing was a guarantee. If something did happen, I was the most senior in that classification and had held that position longer than my peer. I later discovered the official playing rules once I received my official notice.

"I haven't been told anything Ann, "I said, "I am sorry this is happening to you." I wished her a Merry Christmas and we hung up. Following my call with her, I questioned whether I should say something to my boss, and I decided against it. I liked Ann a lot and she is extremely knowledgeable, but oftentimes, she can overreact and make things much more than they really are. I figured it was Ann just being herself and I let it go. I didn't give the conversation much more thought after that.

The day after I received my demotion letter, I received another instant chat message from Ann. She received her official letter just as I had.

"Well…did you get a letter yesterday?" she asked.

"Yes, I did." I typed… *"I really don't know what to think."*

"I think it's bullshit and I know I'm being targeted," she wrote.

What on earth was she talking about? Target? A target of what?

"Why would you think that if some of us are getting notices? This is happening statewide," I wrote.

She went on to explain that she had a history of expressing her opinion on matters and she surmised that this was a deliberate act against her to remove her from her position. She felt she was being targeted and this whole situation was a personal attack against her. While I didn't agree with her outlook on our situation, I empathized with her as everyone handles rejection and hurt differently. She may just need some time to cool down. We ended the conversation on a positive note making a pact with one another that we were in this together and we could be of support to one another though this very undesirable circumstance.

Over the next few weeks, leading up to the date our demotions would take effect, we had a few more conversations in which her demeanor and tone was becoming increasingly resentful and heated. I maintained a positive attitude and outlook on the situation. I had to. I needed to. Not just because the *"Every day is an interview"* mantra was stuck in my head, but because being negative was getting me nowhere. I couldn't afford to stay in a place of anger and blame and resentment on a constant basis. It was hard enough trying to reach for something positive, but it was a deliberate choice I made each day to maintain my faith and wellbeing.

I had hope and faith that there was something more to this than just what it appeared to be on the surface. I trusted that I was being take off a path that was no longer serving me or serving others in a loving light and be placed on a new path where I could shine brighter. I didn't believe that this was how my story was going to end. And, so I chose to believe that I would have a happy ending, whatever that meant. I placed my faith in God and asked him to continue to show me, guide me, in what I needed to do.

It was starting to become uncomfortable for me to engage in conversations with Ann because she was so convinced this was deliberate and everyone around her was out to get her. During one of our conversations through instant chat, I finally called her out on her nonsense and laid out a challenge for her to think a little different. While I truly wanted to be helpful, I could feel my patience wearing thin as she went off again on this being some act of vengeance and a plot against her. I had been supportive, kind, and compassionate and gently offered suggestions that I was doing to perhaps help her too, but they were all disregarded and dismissed. She wanted me to agree and buy into her theory and protest this action along with her. I wasn't about to budge on my feelings and agree with her theory.

My fingers couldn't type fast enough as I wrote one final plea: *"Have you ever considered there might be another reason this is happening? Maybe there are other opportunities out there that we don't know about that is using this circumstance to prepare us for? Maybe, just maybe, there may be some truth to everything happens for a reason, and while that sounds so cliché and I want to gag while typing it, what if we learn of something bigger behind all of this…something so much greater than we could possibly know? What if for one moment, you trusted that this situation was happening for you because there is something it is preparing you that is even better?"*

I hit the send button and exhaled deeply. Part of me hoped she would be open to another perspective, so we could keep our word to one another to be a support system to one another, but the other part of me felt defeated. I had my own energy to protect and her conspiracy theories were a complete drain on me.

As I somewhat figured, she wasn't buying into it, as I saw the tiny dots immediately begin to blink in the reply box alerting me she was responding. *"Nope,"* she wrote. *"Something is going down and I will get to the bottom of it, even if I have to drive to the State Capital and demand a meeting."*

I shook my head at her response, feeling disappointed that I wasn't able to help her see things differently. I then made up an excuse that I had to sign off, which I did. I had tried my best to help her through her mess while going through my own. Some people just don't want to be helped and would rather stay miserable in their own skin rather than be open to seeing beyond their own crappy circumstances for a better way. I can appreciate that there is a wide range of emotions that accompany a setback, including anger. I have first-hand experience. However, I chose to make anger work for me not against me.

You can either allow anger to debilitate and infuriate your mind while wasting precious energy plotting revenge or you can draw inner strength from your anger and take positive action by exerting that energy toward something you find passion in. Respond with intelligence to the situation. Gather the facts instead of jumping to your own conclusions of why something happened or didn't happen. When you respond with intelligence to a situation in a peaceful and professional manner, that does more for you in the long run than an impulsive reaction and say something that you might later regret. The following steps helped me navigate my emotions and vetted my feelings in a healthy and positive manner.

STEP ONE: DEPERSONALIZE THE SITUATION

When we are faced with a setback, it is easier to argue the reality of the situation and begin to believe the conjured story we have created in our minds about our circumstance. That story typically places us in a victim based frame of mind that everyone around us is out to get us. Unless you created this situation with a major rule infraction, or something that would be unethical in your place of work that would warrant discipline or termination, depersonalize the situation. It has nothing to do with your character or the work you were performing.

Despite what we tend to believe as reality to what we might believe, arguing with the facts of the situation is a total waste of time and energy.

It is not our reality that causes us stress; rather, it's the story we make up in our minds about our realities that causes the stress. When we stay stuck in our story, we read more into the situation, justifying the motives and make assumptions about our situation and likely, it's hardly rooted in reality. Instead of harboring negative feelings that will just get you more of the negative energy you are putting out, conserve your precious energy, recognize the lesson, understand that it's not an attack on you, and respond gracefully in ways that will help, instead of hurting your career.

STEP TWO: CHOOSE YOUR RESPONSE WISELY

Viktor E. Frankl wrote in his book, *Man's Search for Meaning*, "Between stimulus and response, there is a space. In that space is our power to choose our response. In our response lies our growth and freedom." Our reputations and attitudes follow us wherever we go. Especially in the corporate world. Anytime we leave one job and start another, our reputations follow us through our previous employers, though a nice little process called reference checks and performance reviews.

When we react to circumstances beyond our control in a gracious manner, that is noticed and respected, and sometimes it is the very characteristic that can land you your next job or big opportunity. Keep in mind that someone is watching what you do after your setback and how you handle adversity. Like it or not, we are all role models. It's up to each of us to choose the kind of role model we will be and how we handle difficult situations. When we respond with intelligence to a situation in a peaceful and professional manner, that does more for you in the long run than an impulsive reaction and say something that you might later regret or impose more damage to your reputation.

STEP THREE: STOP RESISTING THE CHANGE

We inevitably want control and do things our way, so we seek out ways to change the situation. The fact remains that there are some circumstances that are beyond our control than cannot be changed. We fight this internal battle within ourselves that get us nowhere that creates inner turmoil and mounting stress. When we can't change a situation, we must be willing to change ourselves. That includes surrender. That includes becoming willing to be uncomfortable to get out of our own way and patterns that got us stuck in the first place so that we can release what isn't serving us to move on to something bigger and better.

Part of the essence of our professional lives is that it's unpredictable. Nothing is permanent, things continue to evolve and change, and a lot of things can happen that will transform who you are and have an impact on your life. When we develop the practice of viewing each situation with a positive mindset, instead of a defeatist outlook, that is when we begin to cultivate acceptance easier instead of resistance. **Accepting change is a choice, certainly a hard one at that, but a choice nonetheless.** There are two ways of navigating a challenging circumstance: accept what is happening and allow your heart and mind to be open to the positive, or fight against it, be miserable, and struggle against the flow of the Universe.

STEP FOUR: KEEP AN OPEN MIND

When we keep our minds open, we are keeping ourselves open to potential opportunities. If we stay closed minded, we are essentially closing ourselves off from the flow of opportunities that the Universe wants to deliver. When you have a closed mind, it's easy to rush to conclusions. You pass judgment because you believe that there is only one answer or one solution in any given situation. You take the first thing that enters your head and establish it as fact.

One of my favorite quotes by Nicholas Boothman is, "Stay open to opportunity -- you never know where your next important connection will be made." Following your setback, allow yourself to be open and welcome in a reversal of fortune. When we truly feel in our hearts that we have served our organizations well and have delivered on the mission time and time again, use your setback as your setup for the next incredible opportunity that will come your way if you get out of your own way and allow your mind to be opened and expand with limitless possibilities.

STEP FIVE: REFRAME THE SITUATION

Reframing is a method that is used to change your projection on a situation. While we might be able to control our circumstances, we do have ownership and control to the way we respond to what is happening around us. When we reframe our perspective of a grim situation, we not only begin to build our resiliency, but we also can see obstacles as an opportunity. Once we begin to expand our perspective with a positive reframing mindset, we are able to see more opportunities before us getting us one step closer to where we are mean to be.

A positive reframe is taking our situation and finding the good within. While it seems easy enough to do, practicing it can be challenging to do. It's a process that one should practice on a regular basis for the mindset shift to become effective. Two people can have the same exact experience but have two differing takeaways from the situation with a completely different perspective and interpretation of the facts as what happened with myself and my co-worker Ann. That is the power of reframing.

Recognize and Reflect:

1. Reflect on a circumstance that happened to you in which your response to the situation could have been handled more productively. How would you handle that situation differently today by applying the reframing method?

2. In what ways have you suppressed your emotions following a setback and not effectively allowed yourself to self-express in a safe space?

3. Describe an instance in which you responded impulsively to a situation without gathering all the facts. Would your response have changed once you were aware of these?

Every time I thought I was being rejected from something good, I was actually being redirected to something better.

- Steve Maraboli

Chapter Four

REJECTION IS REDIRECTION

"This is the part where you find out who you are."

- Unkown

Rejection hurts. We all want to be accepted and needed, in our personal lives and professional lives. When rejection happens, it can make us question our self-worth and we become critical of ourselves for having been rejected. It takes a toll on our psyche and can really trip us up if we let it. Rejection also has a way of teaching us lessons and perhaps placing us in circumstances that are the right time and place for a specific reason.

Two weeks after I had received my demotion letter, I was in my bedroom folding laundry. It was quiet throughout the house and my focus was still on processing my news, rather than wondering where the missing socks were. I then became distracted by a noise coming from the wall behind me. I turned around and noticed my Post-it note that read, "New opportunities at work" was starting to peel away from the poster board. Then it gently lost its grip, peeling away completely, and floated to the floor. I went over and picked it up and held it in my hand for a moment looking at the words I had wrote before crumpling it up and walked it over to the trash to throw away. I turned my attention back to folding laundry when an idea suddenly took over.

I immediately remembered the vacant supervisor position within the adult services division just before the announcement of the RIF. The deadline to apply had long already passed, but my mind began to list out a number of potential possibilities. Maybe there haven't been interviews yet. Maybe there wasn't enough candidates and it will need to be reposted. Maybe that position will be open to someone who was displaced. It all made sense in my mind. I grabbed the cube of sticky notes and wrote out the words, *"Become the new Adult Services Supervisor."* This time I taped the note to the poster board in the empty space created by the *"New opportunities at work"* falling off. I thought if I shifted the energy and became more specific this time, something different would happen.

The next day at work, I inquired by sending a sincere e-mail to human resources about the position and was informed that the interviews had already been conducted, but should the panel not be satisfied with the candidates, they would repost and re-interview. I had hope and I held on to it. It was the last chance I had before my demotion took effect. I watched the vacancy postings each day hoping to see something come through, but nothing did. My demotion became official and I still had heard nothing about the position. I kept thinking to myself, no news is good news and maintained hope. Then, a week later, I received news about the position that placed me at the lowest point I had encountered up to that point.

I had taken the day off from work as I was ordered to appear in court to finalize the dissolution of my marriage. As I sat on the witness stand, answering the judge's questions, I glanced across the large empty courtroom at my ex-husband, who sat next to his attorney. My heart and mind were encumbered with so many emotions. Two very difficult, life altering events within one week of one another. The demotion and now the divorce.

When the judge tapped the gavel indicating court was adjourned and the final paperwork was to be signed by all parties, we all left the courtroom together and filed into the small courtroom to sign the documents and obtain copies of our legal paperwork. When we were complete, my ex-husbands attorney shook his hand and mine and parted ways. I walked out of the courthouse with my ex-husband as we talked about my situation at work as he asked if I found out anything more about the position. I had shared with him that there could be a possible lead, but nothing was certain. I told him I hadn't but was still hopeful. We gave one another a hug as he told me he would be thinking of me and hoped it would turn out in my favor. I got in my car to head home and had a full blown cry.

I walked into my apartment and saw my work phone sitting on the table where I left it before heading to court. My intuition told me not to check it, but I ignored it justifying that if there was bad news, I was going to find out sooner or later. In my e-mail, I had a message from my boss, with the subject line of a single one word: News.

I opened the e-mail and read what I feared most:

Kim,

I just received word that the position has been filled. The announcement of the candidate will be shared soon. Wanted you to hear this from me.

- Chris

I sat the phone back down on the table and walked slowly to my bedroom. I sank into my bed and buried my face in my hands. I didn't have any more tears left to cry. I was fresh out of them. I never felt more alone and broken than I did that day. I took a few deep breaths, pulled my face from my hands and looked up to see my post-it note on my vision board staring back at me, but it wasn't like it was taunting me or gloating, it was inviting me in to see something deeper.

I experienced a strong surge of hope sear though my spirit. I kept looking at it, feeling this mounting feeling of hope that wouldn't stop. I knew that the everything on the outside told me it was over and there was no chance and no way what I wrote out would be a possibility now. But, there was a voice, a feeling, a trusting that was starting to appear inside that told me it didn't matter what outward appearances were, something much bigger was at work with this and to have hope. Hold onto that hope and don't let it go.

"We do not see what God sees, for we see what is visible, but God sees the heart."

- 1 Samuel 16:7

The moment you let hope to fill the empty space, it becomes the path for grace to heal the wounds of rejection. Grace means allowing your setback to serve a divine purpose instead of assigning it shame. By staying in the flow of hope, I was one step closer to seeing the reason why I would not settle for outward appearances.

A week following my bump, I knew I had to begin doing something in my new role rather than sit in my cubicle trying to figure out how to look busy and appear to be normal. Nothing about this was normal, but I had to do something productive. I was not at all comfortable using our computer system that had more known issues with it than it did assist with processing casework. That was one of the biggest disadvantages of being a manager, not knowing the intricate details of how the system operated and how to help my staff better navigate a system that was anything but user friendly.

I once shared with my boss this very sentiment about how frustrated I was at times because I didn't know all of the shortcuts or workarounds to help other staff. That was when he asked me, what my job was. I looked at him funny and asked what he meant by that. He asked again, "what is your job function as a manager?" I started to answer him by saying it was to know the system that we do a majority of work in and help mentor staff….and then he interrupted me, with a smile and said, "Your job is to manage people, not programs." Ahhh…..smart guy. He was right. My role was to help lead, manage, and direct staff, not try and analyze every minutiae of a complex system. After that conversation, I turned my attention and focus away from having to learn the system and instead focus on management of employees and their development.

As I sat in my cubicle after staring at the log-in screen of the system, I realized that I should have at least attempted to maybe have some interest in learning it before I was forced into it. I knew myself well enough that I would require some time to become comfortable with navigating the screens, understanding where to look for the electronic paperwork, saving data, and keep myself from having a mental breakdown. The manner in which our agency processed assistance applications had changed quite significantly over the years from when I was in a front line case worker position years before.

Back then, we met with clients face to face, listened empathically to their circumstances that led them to apply for public assistance, and offered them alternate and additional resources. The trend had shifted over the years when we implemented the new system to moving towards telecommunications and electronic application processing. For a person who has prided herself on a career in HUMAN services and social work, the thought of having a computer and a telephone take over human connection was bothersome to me. I loved meeting with clients face to face. It felt like I was truly in a role of service and in alignment with our agency's mission. Nothing brought me greater fulfillment than to meet with a client as a follow-up six months from when I first met them to hear about their success and the pride they had for their own rise.

It was a great feeling to share those success stories and witness the joy, excitement, and sheer pride on their faces. Now, those stories had lost a vital element of human connection as we learned of those stories through a digital ether. My biggest apprehension was performing a role that I no longer felt connected to. I wanted, no, I needed that human interaction and relationship building piece.

I had a conversation with my new supervisor, my former peer whom I helped train. I approached her with an idea that I thought would offer a temporary win-win that put me in a position of helping my co-workers, while offering what I could do and what I was good at, meeting and interacting with people in person for appointments. She thought the idea was great and would allow me to gradually integrate myself back into a caseworker role. It was a relief for me. While I truly did want to meet with our clients, I also used it to further delay learning the operating system. I wasn't in alignment with that role. Not at all. I wanted nothing to do with data entry, spreadsheets, electronic documents, voice mail. I was in alignment with serving and helping others.

The day after my idea was approved and implemented, I received a call from the receptionist letting me know I had my first appointment of the day in the lobby. I literally skipped down the hallway toward the reception waiting area feeling gleefully happy that I didn't have to log-in and complete an appointment over the phone like some robot. I opened the large wooden door that separated our work area from the lobby and observed one person seated in a chair. Process of elimination told me this was my appointment.

"Julie?" I asked toward the lone person in the lobby. The dark haired woman who was in nursing scrubs looked up at me and smiled. She stood up as I introduced myself and extended my hand towards her.

"Hi, I'm Kim, it's nice to meet you", I said, as she took my hand for a brief handshake. She tried to force another smile back. I had her follow me to the small interview room where we sat at a table as I began the interview process with her. As I glanced over her paperwork, I noticed she was a single mom working as a nurse's aide, which explained why she was wearing the scrubs. I asked her if she was heading to work following our appointment, or if she was just getting done with work coming from a midnight shift. She looked down and began nervously twirling the soft brown leather tassel on her purse. She explained that she had just completed her last shift at work and was informed by her supervisor prior to coming to our appointment that it was her last day as there wasn't enough patients to justify the number of nurse aids they had. Since she was the last one hired, she was the first one to be laid off, even though she had worked very hard and was told she would be given a glowing reference of her outstanding work performance.

The tears started to fall from her brown eyes as she whispered softly, "I don't know what I am going to do, I loved this job. All I want to do is care for people and keep doing what I am good at. "Her words landed on me. In her, I saw me. In that moment, I felt her distress and rejection, but at no time during those few moments did her focus shift toward financial fear, which is unusual of clients that I have had in the past. Usually, it's the first thing that our clients turn toward and become super upset about is not knowing where money will come from to pay their bills or place food on their tables. Hence the very reason they apply for public assistance benefits.

This conversation was different. She was more concerned with having to relinquish something that she didn't want to let go of and still viewed her role as a nurse aid as a service to others. As she talked about one of her patients, I could see the spark in her eyes and how happy it made her feel to care for another individual. She concerned herself more with what would happen to her patients than what would be happening to herself. As I sat and listened to her, I felt compelled to share a brief piece of my setback with her in an effort to relate to the hurts she was feeling and to provide hope in that hurt. I had a month to prepare for my hurt and rejection. Julie had no notice at all and was handling her news as far as I could tell, like a warrior, or perhaps she was still in shock.

Out of nowhere, words came from my mouth that quite honestly, somewhat startled me. I explained to Julie that her situation, like mine, was only temporary and that something good would come from what she was going through, she just needed to trust that another opportunity was out there for her and all that was required was for her to have an open mind and open heart. As soon as I finished, I thought to myself, *"Where did that come from?!"* I was still trying to process my own words when she looked up at me, wiped her tears and said, "Thank You, that is really kind of you." We finished the interview and I gave her my business card and told her to contact me with any changes or questions. I stood up, shook her hand again, and walked her back to the lobby area. There was a part of Julie's story I could certainly identify with. The feeling of rejection. While our situations were different, the rejection was real.

None of us are immune to rejection. Whether it is from a person, a relationship, plans, a job, sports, it can be traumatizing if you allow it to be. These experiences are what we make it and how we perceive them to be. Rejection can feel very personal even though we may know otherwise. It's the human part of us to feel needed, desired, and wanted, and when others turn their backs on us, or we are turned down, we question what we did wrong and project that pain inward. A way we can help minimize this pain is to reframe the way we view our circumstances as we learned in the previous chapter. We may not be able to control what happens to us when we become rejected, but what we do have control over is our response to the rejection. Rejection doesn't have to be a negative. When we can turn our attention in a new direction, we become aware of a new possibility that we may not be aware of had the rejection not happened in the first place. Instead of staring a closed door in front of you hoping that it will open again if you knock hard enough, turn around and take notice of the windows of opportunity that surround you instead.

Two weeks following my meeting with Julie, I received a phone call from her. Her voice was more joyful and happy, I almost didn't recognize who I was speaking with. She wanted to share with me that after our meeting, she really listened to what I said, and leaned toward trusting other opportunities would be presented to her. As it turned out, Julie had shared her story with a representative at the unemployment office while filing for benefits. The representative had an elderly family member that required in-home care and was seeking a nurse's aide part-time and Julie's personality and experience fit the needs of what this family was seeking. The pay was double what she made in her former job, she would be working part-time to be able to be home for her children and not have the added expense of child care after school, and the patient's home was less than a mile from where she lived. Julie was so enthusiastic and was so incredibly grateful.

She said, "Thank you for your words." For whatever reason, I felt I was in the right place at the right time. I congratulated Julie and wished her much success. Sometimes, the Universe asks us to wear our wounds proudly as we have earned the wisdom they have taught us and in turn rewards us with a new and better beginning. I hung up the phone and sat back in my chair and smiled. A thought crossed my mind that maybe the words that I was surprised to hear myself say to Julie, really weren't coming from me, maybe I was being used as a messenger of hope. Maybe I was serving in a position to offer hope and be an answer to someone's prayer, Julie's prayer. I thought to myself, if I wasn't demoted, this conversation would have never happened like the way it did. It was that moment that I gave a little shout-out to God for Julie's success and said, if I can be of help to her, who else can I be of help to? I began to believe that I was supposed to serve in this social worker role for a while being a messenger of hope and encouragement.

A few weeks following my demotion, one of my former staff announced that she would be retiring at the end of March of 2015. While I previously supervised her and her position, it was an area that I never performed work in. Our department had to restructure the supervision of special case worker positions a few years after I became a manager. Since one of these specialized positions was related to the functions I was managing, she was assigned to me. She performed work as an adult services worker, providing social work services to the disabled and elderly population. I job shadowed her for several months, so I could learn what she did. I was fascinated by her clients and the work she did as it was true human social work. I made sure to always carve out extra time for her case conferences or offer guidance on how to help her clients in the best manner possible. I looked forward to hearing updates on the clients I had the privilege of meeting when I job shadowed. Supervising her position was one of the favorite parts of my role as a manager.

After she announced her retirement, many people speculated who would take over her position. Shortly before the RIF, our department went through further restructuring placing the adult services unit in a separate silo being managed by a different organizational entity. There was a lot of fear of the unknown with this unit, which I believe is what prompted her retirement to occur sooner rather than later. Like the rest of our office, I had wondered who might take the chance with being supervised by someone not on site and not part of our office, especially in uncertain times.

It suddenly became clear to me who should apply for her position and interview for it. Me! It was brilliant! If I was going to be forced to vacate my position and be thrown into something I didn't want, perhaps this was the opportunity the Universe was giving me to try something new as long as I stayed open to any and all possibilities and opportunities. I suddenly felt re-energized and excited about a potential new position that not only was in alignment with the work I wanted to perform, but it also offered additional pay from weekend on-call duty that would be incredibly beneficial to my financial status as my demotion resulted in a rather large pay cut. As a newly divorced single mom, the extra compensation was very attractive. I went straight to my former boss Chris with my new vision and excitement. I arrived at his office and saw him sitting at his computer with his back turned toward the door.

"Chris?" I asked, "Do you have a minute for me?"

He turned around and saw me standing in his doorway.

"Hey! Yes, of course, come on in and have a seat," he said as he waved his arm to welcome me into his office.

I entered his office and pulled out the chair that was tucked under his desk. He slid the glass candy jar in front of me that was always stocked with the best miniature chocolate candy bars.

"Want one?" he asked, as he took the lid off and helped himself to a Baby Ruth bar.

"Yes, thank you," I replied as I reached in and took a dark chocolate kind.

"So, what's up?" he asked, "how are things going kiddo?"

"Well, as you have probably heard, things are going slow. It's hard Chris. I knew it wouldn't be easy, but I never imagined it would be this difficult to get my bearings and do this type of work again", I said.

"Uh-huh", he said as he listened.

"You know that Debbie is retiring, and her position will be open here shortly, right?"

"Yeah?" he asked curiously wanting to know where I was going with this.

"What if I applied for her position? What if I interviewed and happened to be offered the position? It's a position I have supervised, but never performed, and its field work, which is something I would love to do and know I would do well at. There are a lot of "ifs" here, but if I were to be offered the position, it would open my position, so that the person I bumped can return to her job and do better at it than I can. It would alleviate my former peers to supervise me which is uncomfortable for them. Would I have your support if I applied and interviewed?"

He looked at me with his eyes wide open, and replied, "I never thought about that. It's an excellent idea and yes, would you would have my complete support to apply and interview for the position. Wow...are you sure this is something you want to do though given the uncertainties with the restructure and how this new silo will operate?"

"Chris, all there has been in my world is uncertainty these last two months. I don't know what is for sure anymore and what isn't. All I know is that I don't want to stay stuck in a place that isn't doing anyone any good. I'm not happy and if this position can allow me to work in a position that might provide some hope and while earning valuable experience, it may open the doors to other opportunities I don't even know about yet. Yes, I am sure I want to do this." I assured him.

"Well then," he said, "you absolutely have my fullest support. I will make sure to personally keep you informed of the hiring process so that you can get your application submitted."

I smiled and breathed a sigh of relief. "Thank you," I said. "Thank you for looking out for me. I feel good about this." I felt so much better and excited about this new direction. I took out one of my old business cards and crossed out my demoted job title and wrote underneath my name, the new title of the position I would be applying for. I taped it to the side of my filing cabinet, so no one would see it there as my request to the Universe to feel my heartfelt desire for this wanted change. It felt right. I could feel the vibrational alignment and knew as long as I believed and trusted, while keeping an open mind and heart, new opportunities would be brought my way. This can work for you too. If you believe that the universe is compassionate, we have a loving swell of energy that is always guiding us, then everything that is happening to you, is happening for your highest good.

Three weeks after sharing my idea and vision with Chris, I sat in front of my laptop at home, watching my laptop upload my current resume, followed by attaching a cover letter, and hit submit to apply for the vacant adult services position that had been posted that afternoon at work. I was prepared to act and so I did. The position closed five days later, and my interview was scheduled for the week I would be returning from my vacation. I took a nice deep breath in after I received my confirmation e-mail of my scheduled interview I completely trusted that my rejection was really God redirecting me to a new path that was intended for me. My time had been served in a position that was no longer serving me or others in a productive manner. The door had been closed and when I turned around, I saw a new door open and ready for me to walk through.

After I had that initial conversation with Julie with the advice that came as a surprise to hear me say, I began to tune in and listen to what I said to her and offered that same guidance to myself to help me navigate from the feelings of rejection to redirection. Some of the methods I leaned on are described below.

1. Rejection can be a viable opportunity to redirect ourselves back to who we truly are and who we are meant to be. If you flounder in resentment and anger it leads nowhere and gets you no further ahead. By reinventing ourselves, this can result in making diverse decisions for the highest good of everyone involved. Redirection requires that you trust what has happened and take the lessons you have gleaned from your circumstances into your future.

2. Trust that your situation is only temporary. Most people become stuck in a mental framework that their situation will never change, and this is how it will always be. That's our ego trying to wreak emotional havoc on us. If you adopt a "this or something better" approach to what it is you are seeking, maintain that faith that good will come. Rejection often redirects us toward the right and best path.

3. Rejection can also be a form of protection. When we don't get the relationship we want, or the job we interviewed for, the business deal, or the sale we were hoping for, it can often be a form of the Universe's protection against something that could have gone wrong or that perhaps something better is waiting for us if we stay patient and trust the process. Often we become impatient when things don't happen for us quickly or they fail to evolve altogether. There is a reason this happens. Have faith that the Universe is always guiding you toward your highest good.

4. Take a chance. Sincere opportunities are not common, and they often appear while we are absorbed in our inner world not paying attention when they emerge. Learn how to keep your intuition attuned to something that feels right and then act on it. Have an open mind, embrace the uncertainty, and seize the opportunity when it beckons. Taking risks come easy to some while others, the mere thought of doing something like this would render them in a fetal position. If you have been rejected, chances are, you might already be in a heap on the floor, curled up in a ball. Why not take a risk and try something that feels spiritually and emotionally aligned with what you want?

Recognize and Reflect:

1. Reflect on a time in your past when you may have been the answer to someone's prayer? How did this change your perspective on the situation that you were in?

2. Think of a time when you have felt rejected from a relationship, a job, an interview, or a business deal. In what ways did this experience allow you to see that something else better was behind it?

3. What lessons have you learned from rejection?

*This is the part where you
find out who you are.*

- Unkown

Chapter Five

TAKE A TIME OUT

S tanding in our own way crowds the door for a new opportunity to enter. Our lives are always in transition. We transition from one phase to another, as we age, switch careers, raise children, take vacations, find a new hobby, the list goes on. If we don't complete those transitions in a healthy and wholesome manner, we continue to take pieces of unhealed transitions into the next phase of life, eventually filling ourselves up and not leaving room for newness to enter.

As shared in the previous chapter, we tend to stay stuck relying on our strengths and not paying attention to new opportunities when they emerge. When we stay stuck in resistance, we tend to continue to circulate it around, filling up our vessels with more resistance and not emptying it creating space for that new idea, person, or possibility to come in. There is a beautiful story that illustrates this very point:

There once was a college professor who was interested in learning about the study and practice of Zen. He decided that the best way to do this was to find a Zen master to interview. Being struck with an inspiration, the professor did his research and found one on the Internet by Googling, "Zen Master. "The professor shot off an email and made an appointment. On the day of the appointment at the designated time he shows up at the Zen Master's home, notebooks in hand and his mini–recorder ready to capture the important points.

The Zen master greets him at the door with a slight bow and invites him in. Once he is seated the college professor says, "I want you to tell me about Zen, everything about Zen. I want to understand Zen." He places his recorder on the table and prepares to take notes.

"Yes," the Zen master replies. "Let's have tea."

Slightly annoyed that they weren't getting right to the point, the college professor quickly thinks that it is probably best to be gracious to his host since they were in his home and so he sits back and doing his best to hide his impatience he waits until it is time to begin.

The Zen master brews the tea in a pot and brings out two cups and saucers. He then starts pouring tea into the first cup. He pours until the cup is half filled and continues until the cup is almost completely full. And then, to the college professor's amazement, the Zen master continues pouring and the tea flows over the sides of the cup and into the saucer and still he keeps pouring. Just as the tea overflows the saucer and runs onto the table the professor shouts, "Stop! Can't you see that the cup is full? It can't hold any more!"

"Yes," says the Zen master. "It is just like your mind. It is so full that it can't hold anymore. In order to learn about Zen, you must first empty your cup, your mind."

When we are too full of knowledge and set in our ways, patterns, and behaviors, we become complacent and rigid. We don't embrace new methods of learning or seeking out new processes unless you are forced into the situation. Think about the last time you willfully decided to act on your own and learn something new without it being suggested or forced upon you. How did it make you feel to initiate that thought and then act on it? In some ways it likely led to a feeling of satisfaction, independence, and even a recalibration of your spirit in some sense. If you haven't tried to do this independently, I urge you to be gentle with yourself as you explore new methods and would encourage you to stay curious with the process. If you are actively involved in personal development and already seek new pathways to improvement, I encourage you to continue building your platform for growth and expansion.

Quite often, we are so filled up with things to do, places to be, and decisions to make. Our calendars are filled every day with appointments, meetings, coffee dates, social events, the list goes on. Over time, when we continue to stay at the mercy of our jam packed schedules, our minds become cluttered with ideas, beliefs, and certain mindsets that can seem that we are trapped in a perpetual cycle of an overactive mind, which can led to stress, anxiety, feeling scattered, and sometimes forgetting about things that do matter. We have a tendency to overschedule ourselves, checking the to-do's off our list, oftentimes in autopilot mode, landing at home late, exhausted and depleted. This can hurt us more than help us, especially as we try to bounce back from adversity. When we don't create the space in our schedules for healing to happen after a setback, we remain stuck and further delay the healing process to happen. We must make efforts to create that beautiful space for shifts and expansion to occur in our circumstances, so we can emerge on the other side where we are destined to go.

When we continue to fill our days to keep us busy and avoid the hurt, we aren't allowing a space for loving energy to enter and help us get us closer to where we are meant to be. Once we can physically, emotionally, and mentally shed what is no longer serving us, we then can begin to provide that space for growth and new opportunities to enter.

One way we can give ourselves that time and space is by taking a time out, by removing ourselves from the situation, even if that means changing our physical environment for a brief period of time. Whether you have been at work and experienced a layoff or unexpected job change, if you have experienced a break-up, or anything else that might lend itself to be a constant reminder to you that is now missing, I would suggest changing your environment. This may mean, taking a few days off from work. If this isn't feasible, make sure you are taking your scheduled breaks and lunch periods as they are due to you and changing the scenery of your surroundings.

Four months prior to my demotion, my family made plans to travel to Myrtle Beach for Spring Break. I used to be horrible at giving myself permission to take scheduled breaks and oftentimes worked through my lunch periods. When I would depart from the office, I would walk out into the parking lot and see only a few cars because it was well after 5:00. Does any of this sound familiar? However, even though I knew I was exhausted, I had been looking forward to taking my children on our first "official" Spring Break trip that involved sunshine and sandcastles and not a staycation with snowbanks. The trip had been paid for with the exception of expenses that would be incurred to and from our destination along with any incidentals while we were there. With the jarring news of my setback, along with my divorce being finalized, I had forgot all about our vacation until I received an automatic confirmation e-mail a month before. I debated whether or not I should take this trip. With the huge pay cut and uncertainty surrounding my finances, I wasn't sure if I wanted to spend some of my savings on this venture.

My mother, who was quite versed in this territory for years as a single mom herself while raising me working two jobs told me point blankly, *"You need to go."*

I was surprised to hear this from her as she typically is a little more reserved when it comes to spending, especially when there are hardships in place.

"Seriously?!" I asked acting rather surprise and more so wondered if she lost her mind. *"You think I should still go?"*

"I think you need it and the boys need it," she said. *"It'll be good for you to get away from all of this for a little while. You will have us there to help with the boys and anything that might come up on the way there and back."*

She was right. I did need it. I needed the mental break. I hadn't taken any time off to myself to fully process my demotion. In some ways, I had a fear based story around missing work. I thought that if I left work for a few days, I would miss out on new information or opportunities that would surface during my leave. I dismissed that story and decided to leave work at work and take the time that I needed. I had already scheduled the time off and had also just submitted my application for the adult services position that had been posted. As the date grew closer for our vacation to start, I could feel my readiness and anticipation growing. I had a dream a few days prior to leaving that was very vivid and I was recounting details from it the next morning which I typed into my phone, which is an anomaly as I typically don't recall my dreams. This one was different though and it stuck with me.

I dreamt that I wandered out to the beach to watch the early morning sunrise. A long wooden pier stood to the left of me with white nautical flags attached to each of the posts along the pier. The sky had a soft warm glow to it with a small circular shape of vibrant orange that was beginning to emerge from the horizon. Although I was on the beach alone, I felt a loving presence with me that assured me everything would be okay. I knew in my heart, it was God that was placing that assurance in my heart, keeping me close, letting me know He was with me. It felt safe.

The Friday before I left, I received a call for my interview. It was scheduled for the Tuesday after I returned from vacation. I felt ready for a new beginning and a fresh start. Going on vacation would most certainly jump start that.

When we arrived in Myrtle Beach, we couldn't wait to head outdoors and soak in the sunshine and nourishment from the ocean air. I watched as my children approached the Atlantic shoreline for the first time and reached down to touch the water. This was our first time seeing the ocean and we did it as a family. It was a surreal moment absorbing their reactions and witnessing their first experience with a sea of salt water. The thought of work never crossed my mind. I was captivated by my surroundings and finally could feel myself begin to relax.

Each morning, I was the first one awake and out on the beach to watch the sunrise. The first morning, I looked for the pier in my dream and saw one pier to the South of our condo way in the distance, about 3 miles away. I laughed at myself thinking that I would somehow re-enact a dream of a place I had never been to before. I used my mornings as my time-out with myself.

I took time each of these mornings by sitting on the beach with my focus and gaze on the sunrise, having a conversation with God. I prayed and meditated listening to the birds and the waves crashing into the shore. After the sun had risen, I would take a short walk or sometimes run along the beach allowing myself to release emotions. I gave myself permission to feel anything that might come up. Even it was lingering anger, frustration, disappointment, grieving a loss, or a celebration of the work I did accomplish. I knew I needed to do this as a critical part of my healing.

What we can't be with will dominate us. We hold the door closed on emotions and scars, not allowing those to move through us. At some point, we have to become willing to relinquish the old story. We must make an intentional and deliberate decision to stop relying on the past. We use this as our defense mechanism and excuse to warrant behaving and feeling the way we do. The more we compare the past to the present, the more it will continue to show up for us over and over again. We become addicted to this story because we feel we are entitled to our thoughts, beliefs, and opinions because it's safer to discharge blame and shift that responsibility onto someone or something else as opposed to taking ownership for the way we feel.

We have to create the space in that story to open the channels and allow release. This is where growth and healing happen. By allowing these things to move within us and through us, we can stop victimizing and keep noticing. The source of our creation is inside, not out. Beautiful growth happens in some of our darkest and weakest moments.

Think of a time out as an update to your operating system. Many of us have smart devices that require updates to their operating system to ensure efficiency and work the glitches out. We are very similar in nature that we require a routine recalibration of our operating system to make sure we are functioning in our best capacity. We most commonly do this in the form of self-care, which can be anything you decide is best for you.

For me, having this time away from my job and my home was a way in which I could create time and space to update my system and begin to shift into a new frequency of positive and supportive energy that was guiding me to a different path.

The final day of our vacation, we weren't quite ready to depart from the beautiful temperatures of sunny South Carolina. We decided that we would stay for one more day before making the journey home. The condo we had rented was not available, so we had to relocate to a different hotel for one more night. Upon arrival, my kids noticed the nice outdoor pool and that is where we spent the rest of the afternoon. I didn't step out onto the beach until the very next morning when I woke up early again to catch one more sunrise before making the trip home. There was something very cathartic about watching the sun rise each morning and as much as I love sleeping in on vacation, I was more committed to witnessing the sun rise above the horizon each morning. In some ways, I looked at each day as a new beginning. An opportunity to start over again each day, one day, one moment at a time.

My alarm on my phone gently alerted me it was time to get up and head out to the beach. I stepped into my running shorts and pulled my sweatshirt over my head as I threw my hair in a messy bun and slipped into my beach flip-flops. I grabbed my phone and room key and quietly snuck out to not wake anyone.

I made my way down the concrete pathway and stepped onto the cool sand and started to make my way toward the shoreline. And then I saw it. I stopped, gasped, immediately got goose-bumps, and then felt tears in my eyes.

Off to the left side of me, was a long wooden pier adorned with white nautical flags blowing in the gentle warm wind. I looked out over the horizon and saw the shape of a vibrant orange circle slowly making its debut for the day in a clear, warm sky. I stood there in awe as I was looking out and around. This was the dream I had. All of it. I was all by myself and could vaguely make out people off in the distance. The sunrise was all mine to experience that final morning. I smiled and made my way close to the pier watching the waves roll into the shore. As soon as my toes touched the water, I felt it. I felt that loving energetic presence all around me as I had experienced in my dream. I was completely surrounded by the most beautiful and peaceful feeling that I had searched for. Unequivocally I knew in that moment I would be okay, more than okay. This was definitely the beginning of something much bigger than me at work. I stood there just allowing it to fill me up for as long as I could before the sun was high in the sky and I knew it was time to return to my hotel room to begin packing and start our journey home.

As we drove home, I mentally sorted through the different pieces of our vacation. Watching my children experience the ocean for the first time, my mornings spent in solitude with the sunrise, picking up seashells from the beach, and exploring under the piers. This time away had truly been the biggest blessing for my spirit. I felt refreshed and revitalized. While this time out was certainly a welcomed break and temporary detachment from my circumstances, I also realized that this wasn't by any means a cure for the anxiety, stress, or uncertainty I was under. What was needed was a shift in perception. It's quite difficult to gain clarity and awareness in an arduous circumstance while paying attention to internal changes when your nervous system is under attack.

Removing yourself from the situation, taking a step back and watching from the sidelines can actually be valuable. It gives you the benefit of seeing both sides impartially. I remember thinking to myself following my demotion, just sit and be aware of the new dynamics that are occurring. I had been in both a player and coach role, now it was time to be the spectator. Merely observing from the sidelines having the knowledge on both sides is a rather unique position to be in. If you find yourself in a position similar to this, use this as an opportunity to learn and grow. I began to restructure my habits and made sure I was allowing myself the time that I needed to get up out of my seat, leave my surroundings altogether, and return in a different frame of mind. At 5:00, it was pencils down and computer off. It wasn't a slight against my employer or had anything to do with them, but everything to do with me. I had to rewire my patterns and behaviors for healing and well-being.

I was ready to start over again with something new. I purchased a new outfit for my job interview and had started to prepare for my interview. Having spent the last seven years on the opposite side of the table as a hiring manager, I felt confident in knowing what kind of interview I needed to deliver to make myself stand out and shine. The interview style our agency uses is a relaxed behavioral based interview style. Since the position I was applying for was considered entry level, I had to reflect on situations that I encountered from when I was a caseworker several years before.

When I returned to work following my time off, my former co-manager saw me as I arrived to the office and smiled.

"Wow! You look different," she said. "You look very relaxed."

"Thanks," I smiled back at her. "I feel amazing and it was exactly what I needed. I am so glad I took that time. I really think it helped me re-evaluate my situation and allowed me to start over again".

"Are you ready for tomorrow?" she asked.

You know, I really am," I said. "I'm looking forward to my interview, so I can share what I have learned and how I can be of true service to others."

She smiled back, and said, "You have always been so good at speaking and conveying your message. I have no doubts that you will do beautifully."

Just before she left for the day, I saw an incoming e-mail from her. It read:

You really do look amazing, that's the person I remember working with. I know all of this has been so hard on you and I'm glad you took some time off. Vacation looks good on you. Now let's continue on this wave of greatness that you feel and land this interview. I'll be thinking of you. Good luck tomorrow!

I was ready. I had reviewed the competencies, wrote down several situations that I had experienced over the course of my career, had mentally prepared my closing statement for why I should be their selected candidate, balancing my assertion between confidence and passion. More importantly though, I was ready because I had intentionally taken the time to nurture my spirit and begin reinventing myself.

The day I had awaited had arrived. It was the day of my interview. I woke up early, so I could meditate and pray before leaving for work, so I could properly prepare my energy and mindset. I sat in stillness and asked for guidance and wisdom. I dressed in the new outfit I had purchased on my vacation and slipped a green aventurine crystal inside my bra.

I stumbled across this gem while visiting a shop along the oceanside. As I walked around the store, the crystal display had caught my attention and as I approached it, the first crystal that I looked directly at was the green aventurine. Not knowing a lot of the healing or energy surrounding crystals,

I was curious about it and why this particular one had caught my eye. I pulled out a small piece of paper that sat under the tray of various shapes and sizes of the gem, so I could read what it was used for. I started to read:

The green aventurine stone is a referred to as a "stone of opportunity" and can provide extra energetic support for job success and interview confidence. It enhances one's chances for any first situation such as a first date or a job promotion. As if that wasn't enough for me to be convinced to purchase one, I continued reading more...

Green aventurine helps release old habits, patterns, and disappointments so that new growth can emerge. It invites in optimism allowing one to move forward with confidence to embrace change. It enhances creativity and motivation and supports perseverance in one's ability to navigate adverse circumstances. Whoa! Yes, yes, and YES! I was not about to leave the store without this and smiled on my way to the check-out at the synchronicity in how precise the universe is in guiding us to what it is we need and when we need it. As I finished getting dressed and made sure my crystal was secure on my person, I took a nice deep breath and said, "Okay, Kim, let's do this."

I arrived at work just prior to my interview and noticed as I stepped into my cubicle, a lovely bouquet of flowers sitting on my desk. They were from my ex-husband. He had sent them to wish me good luck on my interview. He knew how difficult this had been on me and only wanted the best for me and for our children. An hour later, our secretary came to get me and take me to the board room where the interviews were being conducted. My former boss, Chris, was one of the panel members, but I made sure that I treated this interview as though I was meeting him and speaking about my work history like it was the first time he had met me. The interview started, and the three panels members took turn asking questions. I made sure to take my time with my responses to properly convey the message that I was the best person to serve in this role. I was articulate, passionate with my delivery, and truly felt this was one of my finer interviews as it was done from the heart. I concluded with my closing statement reaffirming my desire for the position and was gracious in thanking the panel for their time for listening. I shook their hands and left the room feeling the most confident I had felt in a long time. I had done my part. It was now time for me to exercise patience and wait for their decision.

A week later, I received the call I had hoped for. I was offered the position in which I gladly and happily accepted. This wasn't just an offer for a new position, it was an invitation for a new beginning. I hung up the phone and silently rejoiced offering a prayer of gratitude. My new job would begin in two weeks. I was giddy with excitement and ready to embrace a new challenge that would allow the gifts I had to offer to be utilized in a new role.

There are times that we have limited influence over circumstances and situations that are beyond our control. However, we do have the capacity to take back our personal power from the very thing that is dominating and occupying space in our minds that doesn't deserve to settle there. Your environment is an important piece of you and your identity. When we can remove ourselves from our surroundings and take the time to reinvent ourselves with compassion, love, and patience, it helps create a new part of who we are and reinforces the person we desire to become. When we become motivated enough to take back our authority, we not only become fierce, we become free. This is the art of starting over.

Recognize and Reflect:

1. Think of a situation that has caused overwhelm or loss. Were you able to remove yourself from that environment for healing to occur? What happened? What would you do differently now?

2. List three ways that you can begin implementing self-care methods into your daily routine?

3. In what ways have you changed your patterns or behaviors to create space for growth?

*You've got to tell your money what
to do or it will leave.*

- Dave Ramsey

Chapter Six

LET'S TALK MONEY

When I began my search for a book or blog on navigating my way through a setback, I was also on a mission to find information on what to do when financial hardship strikes, in which I was unsuccessful in my quest. I know there are plenty of books and blogs on this subject that exist, but because I was too hyper-focused on the looming lack of my resources rather than what was working for my highest good, I was actually blocking any help or guidance to be brought to me. It wasn't until I surrendered and leaned strongly into my faith that I could release the fear of financial struggle, take the pieces of what I was learning and applying them, and then begin to heal my relationship with money.

To help assist you further in your journey in this book, I have outlined eight steps I took to turn my financial situation from being concerned to being confident. The biggest thing to remember is that your circumstances are only temporary. We all have an inner critic that likes to show up uninvited to our pity parties and like a bad guest, not knowing when to leave. Our inner critic enjoys telling us things that can trip us up like the cartoon devil that sits on our shoulder whispering bad advice or telling us it will never get better. When we can begin to rely on the angel on our shoulder instead and stay in faith, our circumstances will turn around. Nothing lasts forever.

Thankfully I had a force of loving support on my shoulder that was able to silence my inner critic. My mom. If anyone knew a thing or two about surviving financial hardships, it was her. For many years, she worked two jobs herself as a single mom after she and my dad divorced. She was conscious of her spending, saved for emergencies, and knew a thing or two about hustle and hard work. Her work ethic and devotion to serving others in a teacher capacity laid many foundations for those in her path, including her own daughter.

When I first told her the news of my demotion, I was standing at my kitchen table with my pile of bills that I was getting ready to pay. She was empathetic and genuinely sorry for what had happened, and then, without skipping a beat, she didn't waste any time busting through her parental boundaries and opened the conversation regarding my finances.

I immediately was transported back in time to high school after just receiving my paycheck from my first summer job. I was standing in our kitchen when she cornered me and asked me how much was check was and what I planned to do with it.

"How much is your check?" she asked me.

"$144.17," I proudly declared as I showed her my first official check while smiling.

"I hope you are planning on saving everything but $20.00 from your check. You do plan on putting the rest in savings, right?" Her question tried to sound like she was giving me a choice, when really, she was more or less telling me what to do.

"Save it?" I asked her as I scrunched up my nose. "I was hoping to buy a new pair of Keds and the new Paula Abdul tape."

"We don't have a shopping trip planned for a few weeks, so that will give you time to decide if it's something you want or something you must have, so you might as well save it for the time being," she told me. We lived in a very remote area that didn't have access to a lot of shopping and we had to plan our shopping excursions pretty meticulously. Seriously, where was Amazon prime when I was 14?

I let out a disappointing sigh and ended up depositing my entire check that summer day, with the exception of $20.00 so I could spend it on ice cream, soda, and pay my way into our community summer dances. Flash forward 26 years later standing in my kitchen holding a similar conversation.

"So, how much will your check be now?", she asked me as I sorted through my bills. Like I said, she busted right through her parental boundaries and was waiting for me to respond to her as though I was 14 again. This time, I didn't want new shoes or an iTunes card. I just wanted to be able to pay my rent and keep the lights on.

"I'm not sure mom," I explained. "With all the deductions I have coming out with health care, vision plan, flexible spending, retirement, and my 401k, I don't know exactly what it will look like for sure. It's roughly an $800 loss each month."

"First thing you need to do is stop contributing to your 401k," she firmly said.

"What?!" I exclaimed.

"You heard me", she said. "Suze Orman says, 'People first, then money, then things.'"

I looked at her with massive doubt in what she was saying to me.

"I'm serious," she said again firmly, and then I knew she meant business. "Taking a few months off from contributing to your 401k isn't going to do any long-term damage. You are going to need the extra money in your paycheck until you begin to figure out a new budget."

I took her advice and made the change to my contribution immediately so that the change would take effect around the time my paycheck would reflect the loss of my income. Recovering from a financial setback may be difficult. It may bring up feelings of shame, embarrassment, and fear. While these are perfectly normal feelings to experience, trust that you can recover from this, even if it doesn't feel like it at the time. In addition to taking my mom's (and perhaps Suze Orman's) advice, here are the steps I used to recover quickly from my financial setback.

STEP ONE: CHANGE YOUR PERSPECTIVE

Changing your outlook on your situation is the first step in getting through this setback. Difficult circumstances don't last when we change our perspective toward them. If you continue to make excuses about your finances, telling yourself this is the way things are going to be, or how broke you are, or that you can't afford your bills, then you are thinking with a broke mindset and will eventually become a self-fulfilling prophecy that will be hard to break away from. Remember, your thoughts manifest into form. So do yourself a favor and begin to intentionally change your thoughts to thinking and feeling abundant. Be willing and more importantly, open to receiving plentifully. You don't need to figure out the how, that will be shown to you.

One of the best things we can do to improve our outlook on money is to lean into the surrender of "I don't know where it's going to come from, but I trust that it will." I realize that this may stir up some feelings of doubt. Our minds are attached to certainty and specific outcomes. When these don't go the way we believe they should, it causes fear, worry, and despair to increase. Once we begin to shift away from negative patterns of our beliefs around our financial status, it is then we can slowly begin to open the floodgates for abundance to enter.

If you are being brought to this, trust that you will be brought through this financially. Being rooted firmly in positive belief that your situation will turn itself around is the cornerstone for much quicker success. The more you lean into this and fully believe and trust it, even though it may not look like it from the outside, incredible shifts begin to happen. Miracle moments happen each day. Trust that they can and will happen for you too.

STEP TWO: CHANGE YOUR RELATIONSHIP WITH MONEY

Each of us are closely connected with money. Whether we are earning it or spending it, it is a part of our lives. Many individuals have an unhealthy relationship with money that isn't their fault. It's the way you were taught to think about and treat money growing up. Some people have encountered bad experiences with money and as a result, they have carried that around with them their entire lives. Rather than inheriting money, what they have inherited is an unhealthy relationship with it.

To begin to understand your relationship with money, let's start with some essential questions involving it. Begin by thinking of the way in which you view money. Does it flow easily into your life, or do you find that its often a struggle or involves hard work to gain it? Next, think about what comes up for you emotionally when you think of money. Are they feelings of appreciation, gratitude, excitement, and abundance? Or do they typically involve feelings of concern, apprehension, lack, or jealousy? Do you tend to believe that you are taken care of, that your needs are met, and you always have more than enough? Or do you feel that despite how much money you have, it will never be enough?

Clearly identifying your feelings towards money helps you better understand your relationship with it and make necessary changes to attract more. Money is a form of energy, like everything in life. Everything is energy, even our relationships. When we begin to shift our energetic emotions toward money from one of lack to one of abundance, it is then we begin to open the channels and allowing ourselves to receive and have more. This can be done by affirming to yourself that you are worthy of receiving financial prosperity and abundance for the great work you do in this world. When we stay in an energy flow of appreciation for all that we have, we begin to attract even more.

The universe we live in is limitless with the energy of abundance that is available to us at all times. Where we get caught up is when we begin to focus on what we don't have that dictates our capacity to receive. If we are continually aware of what it is that we don't have yet, these feelings will continue to block the abundance we are trying to welcome in. Place more of your awareness on the presence of money than on the absence of it. When we can align our thoughts with the feeling of already it having it now, the financial abundance you so richly deserve will manifest into form.

STEP THREE: ADJUST YOUR LIFESTYLE

We are all creatures of habit and live up to our means. When we earn more, we tend to spend more. When you lose income though from a job loss, demotion, or a divorce, it is more difficult to adjust to that change in lifestyle. It will be a hard transition going from what you know and trust that will be there every month to the unknown of how much or even when the income is coming in. This is where maintaining a positive outlook is the foundation for you to build from.

Changing your habits to align with your new lower income is going to require some work and establishing new behaviors. This may mean you have to plan and prepare your own meals, rather than going out for dinner. Clipping coupons and purchasing things while they are on sale instead of paying full price. You would think that is a no-brainer, but I know several people who purchase something full-price while something similar is on sale right next to it and don't think twice about it. If you are like this, it may be time to re-evaluate those behaviors. The same goes for looking for clothing on discount racks or scoping out the clearance bins first before hitting the shelfs.

Another concern with losing income is the social factor. Just because you have had a loss in your income doesn't prevent you from participating in social events or enjoying entertainment. However, you may need to adjust the forms of entertainment that you were once used to. Look for free entertainment in your communities to take part in. Instead of hitting the movies or a sporting event that has high ticket costs with them, consider heading to your local park, boardwalk, or beach. Most communities have free music or entertainment events happening. Be on the lookout for something creative and yet fun. There is always something going on. It might not be what you are used to, but neither is your new income, so to make the best of your situation, find a way to adjust to your new lifestyle. In doing so, you may be pleasantly surprised that you learned something new or found a new favorite place to hang out that you may not have experienced had this circumstance not happened. There is a lot of truth behind everything happens for a reason. Stay open to the process and be gentle with yourself as you learn and apply new behaviors.

STEP FOUR: KNOW WHERE YOUR MONEY IS GOING

Keeping track of where you are spending your money is similar to keeping track of where a toddler stashes their supply of cheerios. The difference is when you ask a toddler where the Cheerios are, they can identify and pinpoint every nook and cranny in your living room where they hid their tasty morsels. When you ask an adult where they spent their money, they have a blank look on their face, knowing that it's out there someplace, that they did in fact spend it, but can't exactly tell you what store or on-line purchase they made. This is where keeping track of your money and how you are spending it is crucial to your budget.

One way to know where your money is going is to write down everything. You may want to keep track in a notebook, so you can easily observe your spending habits. In one column keep track of your set expenses each month, like your mortgage, rent, auto payment, insurance, utility payments, etc. In another column, list out fluctuating expenses, such as groceries, household and personal items, gas or public transportation expenses. In the third column, list incidentals that you spend, everything to a Starbucks coffee, to the soda out of the vending machine, take-out pizza, right down to the .99 cent pack of gum. If you are more inclined to track your expenses electronically, there are several sites and apps, such as mint.com that is free and is user friendly. By doing this, it gives you a visual of where it is you are spending your money. I would suggest that you review this frequently, especially when you first begin keeping track, so you can look for these extras in the incidental columns that can be and should be eliminated along with ways to reduce the fluctuating expenses. By being conscious of our fiscal behaviors, we gain financial confidence in knowing where we are spending our money.

Several years ago, I came across a quote, *"All too often, we buy things we don't need, with money we don't have, to impress people we don't like."* This is what I like to refer to as 'Keeping up with the Joneses'. Little do we know, the Joneses are likely broke and in massive debt. So instead of being like the Joneses, be like you. Curb your spending, cut out extras, and eliminate unnecessary spending. You may have to ask yourself if it's really necessary to have both a landline and a cellphone. Do you really need cable or satellite television? You will know by looking at your list what this means for you. If you are having difficulty deciding what should be eliminated, then simply ask for guidance for your highest and greatest good. It will be shown to you.

STEP FIVE: CALL YOUR CREDITORS

When I first became aware of what my new, much lower, net paycheck amount was going to be, I pulled my set expenses together, wrote out what I could afford to pay, using this as a back-up plan to advocate for my financial situation. I then proceeded to make phone calls to my creditors. Using this step can be an excellent approach to helping you alleviate anxiety about paying expenses that your former paychecks easily covered.

Start the conversation by explaining your circumstances and then asking what options are available to you. Use the method I took by pitching yourself in a positive way as you would in a job interview by informing them of your loyalty to their company who had been fiscally responsible and has paid his or her obligations on time each month for the last few years. By offering a genuine brief explanation of your hardship status ask them what can be done temporarily to assist you. Most creditors are very good and more than willing to work with you as receiving something from you is better than going into default.

I have to admit, making the initial phone call felt intimidating. I was fearful of being judged, but even more afraid that I would be told there was nothing that could be done. I was wrong on both accounts. The first phone call I made was to one of my credit card companies. I ended up in tears with the customer service representative as I was telling my story for the first time to a complete stranger. She was phenomenal! She genuinely listened, demonstrated complete empathy, and offered me a 4 month timeframe of paying interest only payments, which equaled $18.00 per month.

I went on to make additional calls to my creditors, including my student loan servicer who gave me a 90-day waiver on payments, and to my telephone company, who offered me the introductory customer rate of $19.99 a month as opposed to the $68.00 monthly bill. The calls became easier and easier to make following my initial call. Sharing my story didn't have as many tears involved by the time I finished informing my creditors of what had happened. There was only one company that I ran into some challenges with that I had to use my back-up plan to tell them what I could afford. This was after I was informed they didn't have a "hardship program" available. I called his bluff and told him there are always exceptions to the rules as I explained to him again what I was able to afford. I was becoming good at advocating for my pocketbook. He approved the amount I was willing to pay for 90 days.

When you are first making contact with your creditors, wait to see what they can offer before you have to engage your back-up plan. In my conversations with the creditors, I gained some fabulous insight on what can be done in tough financial times. Creditors will work with you by offering a freeze on payments, interest only payments, debt forgiveness, restructuring payments, the list goes on. All you need to do is make a call, share your situation, and ask for help. This does a few things. First, it provides a sense of responsibility to your obligations and are not ignoring them. Second it shows your creditors that you are willing to try. Finally, it helps with your mindset that your obligations are more manageable for a period of time.

STEP SIX: COLLABORATE WITH YOUR FAMILY

Difficult circumstances happen for everyone and when this occurs, people typically turn to their families for help. Our parents, children, and siblings are the most important people in our lives. They know us better than we know ourselves sometimes. Families can offer support and help to you in ways that no other relationship can match. When setbacks and financial devastation strikes, families are the first people at your doorstep offering their help and assistance. People like to feel they are being helpful, so let them, especially your family. These are the people who you trust more than anyone, so let them feel they are being part of your recovery process.

I am not suggesting that this is a time that you borrow money from family. Borrowing money from family and friends can cause more stress and worry, which is what you are trying to avoid. The issue with this is that when your family lends you money, that automatically incites their opinion of what it is you should do with the money. It's just best to leave that alone and apply the steps here. However, gifts of time and service are a form of financial help which families do all the time without realizing it. My mom helped me for several months by picking up my children from school so that I could save money by not incurring an after-school child care expense. When she saw that I was close to running out of household items, such as toilet paper or laundry detergent, she would replenish these things for me, so I could save money that week as a fluctuating expense.

Each Sunday, my dad would invite us over for dinner and then give us fresh fish to take home to have a preplanned meal that week. It saved me from purchasing additional grocery items and also took the pressure off of meal planning for the week, which can be stressful itself! My ex-husband was gracious enough to help me with anything mechanical related on my vehicle and was an amazing support following our divorce and my demotion. He changed my oil, kept up on the regular maintenance, and helped me by putting winter tires on my car so they boys and I would be safe on the roads. These were all things I would have had to pay a mechanic to perform, but when he offered his assistance, I gratefully accepted.

Family and friends may offer to help you in other ways, such as running errands, mowing your lawn, shoveling your sidewalk, and even lending a listening ear. All of these have value to them. Your family wants the best for you just as much as you want for yourself. Allow them to be a part in your successful comeback.

STEP SEVEN: FIND A SIDE HUSTLE

A side hustle is something that brings in extra income aside from your regular job. Several people have one or even two. A side hustle is not the same as a part-time job, nor does it mean you are working for someone else. This is your own venture to generate a little extra income on the side for something you are passionate about or are deeply interested in. It can be anything from painting, designing invitations, planning parties, starting a blog, auto detailer, and the list goes on. Side hustles allow you the flexibility to do what you want, when you want it, and get paid for it.

Prior to my demotion, I freelanced in semi-professional photography. I loved taking pictures and enjoy being behind the lens. The best part of photography was witnessing the smiles and receiving feedback of my clients when I would post their galleries for preview. It filled me up with so much inner joy knowing that my work and creativity was valued and appreciated. I charged minimally for my services because I was just starting out and it was more about helping others. I didn't make a lot, but it was enough to put towards Christmas or back-to-school clothes. Each year, my confidence and creativity became stronger and flourished. I was often told I should be charging more for my work, to which I humbly smiled and offered a thankful response.

Then my demotion struck and I seriously re-evaluated charging more. Following my own steps in the previous step, I changed my relationship with money and gave myself permission to increase my prices and affirm to myself that I was deserving of being compensated for the great work I was doing for others. I then increased what I was charging for services. That year, I had generated three times as much as what I had made in years past. The calls and messages for photo sessions kept rolling in and I took all the referrals I could get. I worked diligently that year and as a result of the belief in my ability to do great work in the service of others, I was open to receiving financial abundance.

Not only did my side hustle provide me with extra income that I was extremely grateful for, but it also provided me with a sense of personal reward. It was something that I passionate about that occupied space in my mind that was centered around joy and happiness. When I was behind the lens, I wasn't thinking about my demotion or the hardship and stress it had created for me. I was riding the wave of excitement. My side hustle was not only productive and lucrative, but more importantly, it had meaning and fulfillment.

If there is something that you have been wanting to explore, or something that ignites that fire of passion in your spirit, I implore you to try a side hustle. It can occupy a positive space in your mind, generating some extra income that makes up for a loss. Stay open to possibilities that can be generated from this endeavor. Many people who have often started side hustles are led to opportunities that can help them go further and provides valuable good and services that the world needs more of.

STEP EIGHT: DON'T GIVE UP

The final step is not to give up. You may experience a few roadblocks along the way that can delay your progress towards recovery. If that happens, trust that the universe is working for your highest good and that reason for the delay, even if it doesn't make sense at the time, it will someday. The worst thing you can do is give up. The ability to keep your focus ahead of you will contribute to your success in recovering from your setback. Positive thoughts alone aren't always the answer in turning your situation around. Maintaining a healthy perspective on your situation, reframing your outlook, and being gentle with yourself are necessary for turning your setback into your setup.

It isn't easy discussing money, especially when we doubt our self-worth when we experience hardships and setbacks. Spend some time reviewing these steps I have listed and compare them to your own circumstances. By applying just one of these steps, it can get you one step closer to regaining your financial sense of well-being. Trust that your situation is temporary and that circumstances always change. When you lean into faith and surrender, shifts begin to happen even sooner.

Recognize and Reflect:

1. How do you react to financial stress?

2. What are some ways you can bring in additional income on the side? What would you gain from this?

3. What strategy can you use to change my relationship with money?

Wherever life plants you,
bloom with grace.

- French Proverb

Chapter Seven

BLOOM WHERE YOU ARE PLANTED

Shortly after I started my new position as an Adult Services caseworker, I subscribed to a daily inspirational e-mail that was delivered each day during lunchtime that featured a quote or a motivational message. When I returned from my lunch break, it was the first item sitting in my inbox waiting for me to read. I treated this as my mid-day mindset reset moment. I loved getting these messages and intentionally took time to carefully read them and absorb their meaning.

I had been spending a good portion of my time outside of the office, in the field, meeting the clients on my caseload, by conducting home visits, introduced myself to community partners, while learning the details of the program I had once supervised. It felt good to do something different and feel as though I was once again doing work that was fulfilling. Meeting with the elderly clients on my caseload, gave me immense satisfaction knowing that they needed that connection with me just as I needed it with them. I felt a renewed sense of joy and purpose in the work I was performing.

One afternoon, after I had returned from lunch, I checked my e-mail and noticed that the quote wasn't there. At first I was disappointed as I became used to reading them as a part of my afternoon routine. I assumed that it might be just delayed and shrugged it off knowing that it would appear when it did. I prepared for my afternoon home visit with an 80 year old woman who was just released from the hospital that needed in home care. I gathered the intake paperwork from the printer along with directions to her home, my ID badge, and car keys and headed out the door, thinking nothing more about the quote.

When I arrived to my client's home, I navigated my way to the back side of an older two story home that was now turned into an apartment duplex. The directions indicated that the door to her apartment was in the back and up a steep set of steps. I opened the screen door to the enclosed porch and noticed a quaint entry way that was adorned with older style Christmas decorations and a wreath that had obvious wear from being there since December and we were now well into April. I knocked on the door and heard a very faint, sweet little voice from inside that responded to come in.

I let myself in through the door into her kitchen and looked around for her to greet me to which no one was there and called out, "Susan? Hi, it's Kim, I'm here for our appointment."

"I'm in the living room, come through the kitchen." responded my client.

As I made my way through her kitchen and into her living room, I noticed that her tiny one-bedroom apartment was decorated inside just as her entry way was with Christmas decorations, angels, and several framed pictures of Jesus that hung on her walls. I stepped through the threshold of her living room and noticed she was sitting in her recliner with a small crocheted blanket draped over her lap.

"Hi Susan," I said with a smile as I introduced myself, "I'm Kim, we spoke earlier today."

"Come on in and have a seat sweetheart," she said to me as I made my way to the chair next to hers.

"It's really nice to meet you", I said to her. "You have a lovely and cozy home. Thank you for inviting me in."

As I sat down and began pulling the paperwork from my binder to begin her assessment, she didn't waste any time striking up a conversation telling me about herself and her recent stay at the hospital. As I listened to her, I glanced around her living room as she pointed out a few pieces of medical equipment she was using so I could take note of what she would need assistance with. As I turned my attention toward her, my gaze was interrupted by a larger photo frame that hung on her wall just behind her chair that held a cross stitched quote in two different shades of red surrounded by small pink flowers that read: *"Bloom where you are planted."*

She saw me staring at it when she said, "I made that in my church group."

"It's really nice, I don't think I have heard that quote before."

"It's one of my favorites," she told me. "It simply means that no matter how bad your situation is, you must appreciate where you are and learn to grow where you are. Your situation will change, they always do, but only after you grow though what it is Jesus wants to teach you."

I felt my heart soften even more than it already was as I listened to this sweet soul tell me this powerful message. "Thank you for telling me this Susan. I will remember it always." I said with a big smile.

She smiled back at me as we started on her paperwork. Once we were completed, I handed her my business card in which she reached out and squeezed my hand and said, "Thank you for coming and being so kind. I look forward to another visit with you."

"The pleasure is all mine Susan," I told her. "I too look forward to returning in a few weeks. Thank you again for telling me the meaning behind your project," I said as I looked up one more time at the framed print behind her. She laughed lightly as I let myself out of her apartment and walked down the steps toward my car. Pink colored tulip buds were beginning to show on her lawn. I hadn't seen them on my way into her apartment and smiled as I thought of the tulips that were beginning to bloom. I got in my car and headed back to the office. Upon my return, I logged back on and checked my e-mail and noticed that my daily inspiration message came through. When

I saw what the quote was, my jaw almost hit my desk. It read: *"Bloom where you are planted."*

No. Freaking. Way! I immediately got chills as I sat there feeling a mix of divine intervention and dumb luck as I stared at my screen. I instinctively knew it was something greater than me at work and this message was clearly an indicator that I was being asked to pay attention. I went back to what Susan had shared with me and knew that my situation was teaching me something that had value and meaning. I was learning the meaning of presence and purpose.

For as long as I can remember, I had difficulty staying in the present moment. I was a person who constantly looked at her calendar flipping the months forward making notes of events and activities scattered throughout the months. When I planned my wedding, I was in auto-pilot checking off my to-do list, booking the venue, hiring a photographer, picking out my dress, keeping in line with what my calendar said, rather than being willfully present and enjoying the experience. The same held true for when I returned to school to earn my higher degree, instead of carefully reviewing the entire outline of the concentrated program, I made note of when I would be starting and then went straight to the last page of the program looking for the date it was expected to finish. The goal was to get in and get out, navigate my way through the process and be done.

Being present wasn't something I was familiar with and because of that, it made me uncomfortable to sit still and just be. When I become demoted, I had no choice after I landed hard to sit there and be still. I had to learn to practice patience and be mindful of where I was, and most of all, to be grateful for what I did have rather than what was missing or why it hadn't shown up yet.

Life is a series of experiences, each one of them makes us better and stronger, even though it may be hard to recognize this when you encounter hardships. Our greatest tragedies are meant to be turned into our greatest triumphs. They aren't intended to hurt us, but rather help us see the other side of what we cannot see or unwilling to see. When adversity appears, it's easy to settle into a defeatist attitude, discharging blame, and casting judgment on those who have wronged you assigning responsibility for your hurt. Our circumstances won't change under these conditions. Our circumstances do not change until we change. If we have been placed in a situation, we must trust we are meant to be there until we learn what it is we need to know. There is great work happening inside of us during this time. We are growing, learning, developing character, and building resiliency. The moment we can shift our perspective inward and learn to serve right where we are, is when things begin to change in our favor.

Ecclesiastes 3 says, *"There is a time and season for everything."* Each of us has the grace to flourish in the season we are in. We know that seasons throughout the year change. The same happens for the seasons in our lives. When we can relax and be content in the season we are in, we have a much greater capacity to learn and serve right where we are meant to be leading us to the next season. This one simple quote, "Bloom where you are planted," allowed me to better understand what was at work inside me. Even though I knew I knew in my heart a new season for me would come, I needed to practice patience and appreciate where I was. God is always arranging the smallest of details and is always working for us on our behalf. The seasons we are in are continually preparing us for promotion to the next.

Two months had passed since starting my position and I had learned fairly quickly how to perform specific duties of my new job. I was excited to monitor my own progress and watch as I improved from one week to the next. As Friday afternoon of Memorial Day weekend rolled around, I received a phone call from my new supervisor, Kevin, who was located on the opposite side of the state. Kevin knew my backstory from my interview and we had many conversations surrounding management, leadership, and departmental changes. I appreciated the relationship that Kevin and I had as he never made me feel insignificant or shame in my circumstances. He always looked for the best in a situation and for that I was thankful for. My cell phone rang, and I saw it was him.

"Hey Kevin," I answered.

"Hey Kim," he said. "I know it's close to quitting time and I won't keep you long, but I have something to share with you and perhaps run by you."

"Sure thing," I replied curiously. "What's going on?"

"Well," he began, "As you know we have just one supervisor for our area, which I don't have to tell you it's too large of an area for one person to cover." It was true. Kevin was the only supervisor for the Upper Peninsula which is similar in size if you pieced Vermont, New Hampshire, Massachusetts, and Connecticut together. It's a good chunk of territory that he had to cover. He continued, "There have been conversations in the last few weeks about adding another supervisor to help cover this area. The conversations have been receiving a lot of support and we finally learned today we received approval to hire another supervisor. It will be placed in your office. With your past experience, would you be interested?"

I slowly melted into the back of my chair as my eyes closed as I absorbed the news. I didn't know what to say or do. All I could think about was the sticky note that I taped on my vision board a few months earlier that clearly indicated this position. I was blown away. "Yes, of course I would be very interested," I replied.

"I figured you might be, but I wanted to reach out and ask anyway. Once we know more specifics, I can let you know," he said to me.

I thanked him for sharing the news with me as we exchanged good-byes and hung up. I was in awe as I drove home reviewing our conversation and how this position just manifested into form as a desire and an intention. I was slowly learning about the power of positive thought, the law of attraction, how thoughts become things, and here was proof of something that I was seeking had made its way into form.

The position was posted two weeks later in which I updated my resume, drafted a new cover letter, and took a deep breath as I hit the button to submit my application. It was time to practice being patient for an interview. I continued to stay in faith and trust that this was part of a larger plan. I received my confirmation for an interview for the following week and began my preparations once again, carefully reviewing my past experiences in leadership. It was an interesting dynamic entering this interview, with a wider lens and different perspective on what leadership now meant to me having experienced what I had been through. I shared with them my unique view through the lens in which I saw myself, but most of all, I shared the lessons I was learning from my experience and how they impacted my ability to become resilient and handle adversity from a place of empowerment. I felt incredibly encouraged after my interview was over that I had shined my light as bright as I could. It was now up to the panel to decide who was their candidate.

As I waited for news about the position, I took a weekend trip to participate in an all-women's half marathon race in Madison, Wisconsin. The weekend event offered several activities including yoga. I didn't own a yoga mat, nor had I ever tried yoga. I really wasn't sure what to think or expect but was curious from my reiki training that incorporated similar principles. Being curious and open minded were the only things I needed as I grabbed a large towel from the hotel bathroom where I was staying and proceeded to the hotel's large conference room. As I entered, there were several other women arriving at the same time with colorful mats tucked under their arm, chatting with one another. I made my way to the back of the room, toward the corner. They unrolled their mats, stretching them out on the floor carefully as I unfolded my bath towel and flung it out away from me as though I was setting up my space at a beach.

I felt a little intimidated when the women around me were beginning to take a seat on their mat and crossing their legs very carefully while sitting with their back straight. My mom, a former pre-school teacher would called this pose "crisscross applesauce". I later learned this was called lotus pose. As I tried to imitate what the others were doing around me, I tried to not make it obvious that I clearly no idea what I was doing. A woman who was set up close by me, moved her mat closer to my bath towel as more women made their way into the crowded space. People were shifting around creating space for the newcomers. The women smiled at me as she made her way closer to me. I returned her smile.

"Is this your first time doing yoga?" she asked.

Either this person was a psychic or I really had the look of "newbie" written across my forehead.

"Yeah," I responded. "I'm not sure really what to expect," I said.

She nodded her head in agreement as she said, "Try not to expect anything and enjoy the experience. You will love it."

"I hope you are right," I said jokingly.

The yoga instructor came out on to the platform stage to welcome all of us. She was wearing a headpiece with a microphone, so the back of the room could hear her. She pointed out three women that were walking around the room that were her assistants. The instructor and her team all wore the same tank style shirt, with the words, *"Attitude of Gratitude"* printed on the front.

The fluorescent lights in the hotel conference room began to dim offering a more peaceful, relaxed environment. *Good,* I thought. This not only feels better, but maybe someone won't see me if I screw up. The instructor began to slowly guide us into a meditation telling us to breathe in slowly and release our breath. We did this a few times together as soft music played in the background. I felt more relaxed with each breath I was taking in and releasing. We then moved into the asanas as the instructor carefully and in detail described which arm went where and what to do with the other arm. She reminded us to breathe and relax as we could into the pose. The assistants were walking around gently placing their hands on participants in a way to assist them in their posture. As we stood in tree pose, I felt I was being watched by one of the instructors. I looked out of the corner of my eye and saw her approaching me.

Crap! I thought, *I'm doing something wrong. Was it the right leg or the left leg we were supposed to root down in the ground,* I thought to myself as I tried to sneak a look at the person in front of me.

The assistant approached me as I whispered softly to her, "I'm sorry, I'm doing it wrong."

"Not at all and no apologies", she said very warmly. "You are doing it just beautifully, the way YOU were meant to. I wanted to offer a gentle and supportive hand on your back," she said as we switched legs. As I moved into the next position, I felt the strength of her warm, yet gentle hands rest on top of my shoulder blades as though she was pulling my shoulders down away from my ears, which I have a tendency to lift them as a stress response. The extra support felt amazing. "Breathe in gently and out slowly," she instructed. "Beautiful," she said. "Be where you are."

As she spoke those words in her soft and warm voice, I felt tears behind my eyes. *Be where you are.* It was so genuine and kind. She stepped away from me as she moved her way onto the next person. Her words landed on me in a way I hadn't experienced before. The message was so simple, yet powerful.

The class came to an end and the instructor told us to lay flat on our mat, in my case, bath towel, for savasana. As I listened to the music playing to conclude the practice, I recited the words *be where you are*, over and over. I felt another shift while laying on my towel. It felt calming and peaceful. For once, I wasn't thinking about what I was going to do after the yoga class, or the race the next day. I was present and absorbing the stillness all around me. And just like that, I fell in love with yoga. I still use these words today as my mantra to be present in the moment. It helps me become centered and focused on what is, not what was, or what is to come.

Be where you are, not where you think you should be. We live in an age of instant gratification and have a tendency to trip over the future of when we think we should have it rather than allowing ourselves the grace to be where we are. When we establish goals, set intentions, recite affirmations, and dream big, we are creating the future we desire, but the test is to practice patience and be where you are, enjoy the season you are in, so the desires of your heart can manifest in the perfect time and order.

I returned to work the following week and was informed that a hiring freeze had been issued across our department until further notice. No job offers were allowed to be made. Since we were a couple of months away from the beginning of a new fiscal year, the freeze would likely last until then, causing even further delay in hiring. I would have to wait to learn my fate about the position I interviewed for. As disappointing as it was to learn this, I had just returned from my weekend out of town feeling empowered with new self-care techniques and a new mantra. I trusted that the delay was for a reason. Instead of being frustrated and getting upset over something I had no control over, I leaned into surrender and did what I knew to do.

Trust the process, trust the timing, and moreover, trust the outcome.

Recognize and Reflect:

1. Think of a season in your life that was uncomfortable.
What did you do to bloom where you were planted during that time?
Would you do anything differently?

2. Describe a time in which your circumstances didn't change
until you changed. What happened?

3. What mantra or quote would you chose to serve as motivation
to be practice being present in the moment where you are?

When you face difficult times, know that challenges are not sent to destroy you. They are sent to promote, increase, and strengthen you.

- Joel Osteen

Chapter Eight

YOU ARE STRONGER THAN YOU THINK

S etbacks can be heartbreaking. It shatters our ego and vision of how we see our path progressing. While we have little control over what happens to us, what we can control is our response. If we stay in a victim based mentality, we will remain stuck. There is no doubt that a setback can create a void in our hearts. The moment you allow hope to enter the empty space, it becomes the conduit for grace to enter and heal the wound of adversity. Our journey is far from over, and with a setback it may just be the detour that leads us to the path we are meant to traverse. When we can rise above it, learn from it, and move forward, we can get back on track and rewrite our future. It takes a shift in perspective, patience, faith, leaning on your inner strength, and tapping into the tools that are available to you at all times.

Life is never short of giving us adverse moments, but that doesn't mean that it is completely out of our control. When I came down from the initial shock of my demotion, I became determined and driven to change the trajectory of my career. I held firm in my faith and completely believed this was not how my story was going to end. I refused to stay stuck in a situation set by someone else's agenda. I took back my power by leaning on my strengths.

Each of us are gifted with different strengths. The VIA Institute on Character identifies 24 key character strengths which include hope, perseverance, and creativity, just to name a few. When our strengths are utilized and applied, they can have a significant positive impact on your life. The VIA classification of strengths indicates that every individual possesses all 24 character strengths in different degrees, giving everyone their own unique profile. You can discover your own profile by taking their free survey on their website. What I appreciated most after taking this survey and reviewing the results of my own profile, was that toward the bottom of my results, I would have a tendency to view these as my weaknesses as my prominent character strengths being toward the top. What is interesting is that the results refrain from labeling the characters near the bottom as weaknesses, but rather strengths that come less naturally and therefore require extra effort in applying them.

We all have the ability to grow stronger throughout our lives by the circumstances we find ourselves in to harness determination and motivation in order to feel secure. However, when traumatic events unveil themselves, we can easily lose sight of those and thereby lose self-reliance. Prior to my demotion, doubt and insecurity started to sneak in. I questioned whether or not I could handle this, but also trusted that God would never hand down a deal like this to me if He didn't think I could brave the storm.

One afternoon, as I was making preparations to move from my corner office into my new cubicle in the middle hallway, I began sorting through the tall steel file cabinets that had held years of the files I had created over the years, and ones that I had inherited from my former supervisor, who served as my mentor when I first became a manager. Some of the manila colored files had her neatly printed handwriting on the tabs and showed signs of gentle wear on them and were slightly faded from time. I went through seven years of client response letters, policy bulletins, employee personnel files, certificates, and awards our team had achieved. I started to place them into to two stacks and organize them by which supervisor would be the lucky one to receive my files. Right then, my thoughts drifted to Andrea, my co-leader, right hand person, and one of my dearest and closest work friends. Andrea and I had been through a lot of circumstances together. Some fun and some not so fun.

We both faced adversity early on in her career after she was initially hired that resulted in a couple of the candidates being upset with her appointment to the position that it became an uncomfortable work environment for a period of time. We pushed through, growing through each phase, which became the framework we built our teamwork on. We hired staff, we lost staff due to transfers and retirements. We engaged our staff with teambuilding exercises, went through a system upgrade, held many crucial conversations, held trainings, pizza parties, experienced office drama, participated in fun unit challenges, and held Christmas parties. We weren't perfect managers by any means, but we were better together than we were as individuals.

Andrea and I were an incredibly strong team and we balanced each other perfectly. Where I would engage in a buzz of excitement, she slowed me down. I had the creativity, the blank canvas, and the dreams. She was my organizer, developer, and dream catcher. Whenever I would share a crazy new initiative or project I was stirring up, she instinctively took out her notepad and started writing detailed notes of how to put it in motion. She never questioned me or my intent. She trusted me. I trusted her. She was my yin to her yang. Now, as I stood in my office pulling files, I realized that I would be losing a very important relationship that contributed to my success as a leader. Things wouldn't be the same for her either. I knew deep down our relationship would be different and that wasn't something I was quite ready for. As I was finishing sorting through the last drawer of the cabinet, I heard a soft voice coming from my doorway.

"Hey," said a female voice. I turned around and saw Andrea standing in the doorway.

"Hi there, come on in!" I said. "You are just in time to take a stack with you," I said jokingly.

She came in and took a seat on my garden bench as I closed my office door behind her. My garden bench had become the preferred seating accommodation over the years for my co-workers, employees, and boss to sit on when they came into my office. I had brought it to the office during the Fall as I ran out of room at my house to store it for the winter, so I purchased a couple of decorative throw pillows and a comfortable cushion for the bench and it never left my office after that. It became a permanent addition to my corner dwelling that added a nice alternative from the standard office chairs that also occupied my corner space. While the chairs that sat across my desk were used on occasion, the garden bench received the most attention. Many conversations have been held by those who have graced the bench. Some conversations incredibly deep and serious, some lighthearted and downright humorous, and toward the end of my tenure in my position, the conversations stemmed from there become more supportive and some of the most meaningful. Including this one with Andrea.

"How are you doing?" she asked sincerely yet with concern as she took one of the pillows and adjusted it next to her. I could feel my vulnerability begin to emerge.

"I don't want this," I whispered. "It just isn't right," I told her. I sank down in my chair still holding onto a manila file that held old carbon copies of my timesheets from fifteen years prior. "I am afraid I am going to fail. I am embarrassed. I'm trying to be strong on the outside while it is just eating me up on the inside." Up to that point, I had put on a brave face and smiled when I walked by co-workers. There was no way I was going to show my weakness even though on the inside, I was a mess.

Andrea sat there for several minutes before she said anything. She supportively held the space for me as I allowed my emotions to pour out. She then responded with some necessary insight. "You are a very strong person. There is absolutely nothing to be embarrassed about. You didn't cause this. You have the tenacity and determination to overcome hardships. The only way I can be strong through this is to watch you be strong." In that moment, she came through in a way I so desperately needed. Andrea had been the light when I became stuck in the dark. She always used loving awareness to help me get out of my own way and see something larger at work. Sometimes the ones closest to us are the ones able to hold our hand and guide us back to our own light.

I smiled at her as I said, "I promise to be strong." She was right that I had nothing to be embarrassed about, even though it did feel shameful to be "involuntarily demoted." In my attempts to show strength on the outside, I wasn't doing a great job silencing the inner critic voice of shame. The power of dialogue with our inner critic can either be the fuel to our fire in achieving success or it can diminish and hinder forward progress for potential. Having the loving guidance and support of people closest to you can help tame these inner voices. I once heard that it's rather difficult to read the label from inside the jar.

Our inner critic is that voice inside our heads that tells us we can't, we shouldn't, we aren't good enough, or we will fail if we try. This is not to be confused with an inner voice that speaks to us with love, compassion, and kindness, gently nudging us along our path. The inner voice I am describing here is critical in nature. It's the voice that expresses disapproval, criticism, and judgement about our actions. It tends to stand in the way of what we want to accomplish, and holds us back from exploring new ideas, experiencing new ways of thinking and doing. This voice tends to want to limit us in our capacity for believing we are capable of achieving what which we desire, therefore weakening our strongest intentions.

My own inner critic used to be quite clever in derailing me from challenging myself and going for more, until I learned how to handle and tame the voice when I first started to run. I had always entertained the idea of running a marathon, thought it would be an incredible difficult, yet rewarding experience, but because of the inner voice of dissent, I never took the initiative to do so. After the time I had spent on building my endurance and distance with running, I decided to take it to the next level to run a full marathon. I registered on New Year's Day 2014 for the Detroit marathon and was excited about challenging myself on a physical and mental level.

Running an October marathon meant that I would need to begin my training in June. That was also the same time I separated from my spouse, as I packed up boxes, moving from the comfort and safety of our home into an apartment with my two boys. It didn't take me long to figure out that my training would not go as planned. Sharing parenting time, with my estranged spouse meant that on the weeks I had our two children, my training took the back seat and I wasn't able to log the mileage I needed to continue building up on my long runs. My priorities were shifted. I had certain expectations from my training and it became increasingly difficult to keep up with the demanding schedule of training.

My inner critic was beginning to chirp rather loudly. *"You will never finish the race and you'll be embarrassed,"* followed by *"You can't keep up with the training schedule as it is now."* then the final straw *"Serves you right for trying to prove something that you're not."* And just like that the shitty committee inside my brain smirked as it said, "I told you so" as I really began seriously contemplated opting out of the race.

I began to play the victim role shifting the blame, started to settle into disappointment and frustration. A few weeks later, my mom and I took my boys to Chicago for a weekend getaway. Even though I thought I had my mind made up about not participating in the marathon, I was still wavering back and forth with the idea when I was approached with a challenge for my inner critic.

I was standing outside of our hotel while waiting for the concierge to retrieve my car from the parking garage, when I started to chat with one of the hotel employees about how lovely the hotel was and in a perfect location for all the attractions. During our conversation, he mentioned that the hotel was noted for one of the preferred places for the Chicago marathon runners to stay as the hotel was along the race course. His comment caught my attention as I casually mentioned that I had been training for the Detroit marathon, but then nonchalantly brushed it off that I had more or less made the decision to opt out. He then threw out a challenge which eventually tipped my decision.

"Do you wanna do it?" he asked.

His question caught me off guard. "I don't know?" I replied. "I did at first, but now I'm not that sure."

"Why you gonna let those voices in your head get you down?" he asked me as though he was my coach. "If you wanna do it, you gotta believe in yourself, go for it."

DANG! Nothing like a wake-up call to have a deep dive conversation with my inner critic. It was time for me to tell her what was about to go down. Just then, my car emerged from the parking garage as the hotel employee opened my car door for me and smiled as he told me, "Good Luck!" We all got in my car as I sat there for a moment smiling this cheesy smile. I had just been handed a new challenge. That challenge was to tell my inner critic, "Thank you for your concern, but I'm going to do this anyway."

There was absolutely no way I was going to opt out now– this was my journey and at that point I didn't care if it took the entire allocated time to run the race, I was in a new mindset, a new place. I came home and started my training again, as imperfect as it was. That part didn't matter. I knew my body was capable of doing incredible physical things, it was my mind that I had to begin working on. With a little more than two months away, I had a lot of work to do. With every mile that I logged, I felt a renewed sense of confidence, building courage, and mental and physical strength.

My last big race before the marathon was a half-marathon in Iron Mountain, a small community, on the Wisconsin border. I participated in this event as I used it for my training regime. As I completed that race, I felt so confident and ready for Detroit. As I was leaving town, I had to take a side street due to a road closure. I was still gushing with pride as I said out loud in my car, "I am SO ready and excited for Detroit!"

I said, "What do you think God? Am I ready to run this marathon?" As I came to a stop sign, I looked at the road signs to see where I was, and there, quite literally, was my sign. I was at the intersection of Detroit Street and Kimberly Avenue. I was stunned! You seriously cannot make this stuff up! I got out of my car, right there in the intersection and took a picture. Spirit definitely has a sense of humor.

The morning of the marathon arrived, and my inner critic was nowhere to be found, until mile 20, when I started to fall behind my pace team. The inner voice started her chatter, *"You'll never catch up, so you may as well just walk the rest of it."* I listened and then dismissed the voice and continued on my way toward the finish line. As I approached the finish chute, I could feel the tears rise in my throat and felt every emotion known to surge through me and around me. I crossed the finish line strong and feeling incredibly empowered. The Universe intended for me to finish this race on my own so that I could witness my own strength and determination as I stepped across that finish line with immense joy and triumph.

Had I continued to listen to the voice of my inner critic and taken direction from it, I would have missed out on an incredible experience in which my strength was further defined and confidence in myself was deepened. The Universe also knew I needed a little intervention from a complete stranger which allowed me to have the conversation with the concierge in Chicago that ultimately swayed my indecisiveness stemmed by my inner voice.

There are a few ways to help ways to help subdue the inner critic voice. While I personally feel that it really isn't possible to get rid of your inner critic as it's with you on your journey throughout your lifetime, there are ways to handle how strong you allow this voice to be. The following three steps are the ways I learned to help tame the naysayer in my mind.

STEP ONE: CULTIVATE AWARENESS

When we develop awareness to the negative thoughts we tend to tell ourselves, we have the power and capacity to change those thoughts into love, kind, and compassionate responses toward ourselves. By developing awareness, you increase your ability to easily recognize the moments your inner critic tries to sabotage you, allowing you to question it, therefore reducing the likelihood that you will believe the thoughts. Treat this step as you would in speaking with a friend who was going through a difficult time and needed your love and support. You wouldn't speak to your friend in a harmful or hurtful way as it would inflict more pain. The same holds true for us. Speak kindly to ourselves as we would to our friends.

STEP TWO: STOP COMPARING

Comparing ourselves to others can be detrimental as we grow and transform. Agapi Stassinopolous says, "Comparison is an addiction to losing". Comparison is typically the quickest way to reach unhappiness. All it does is keep you focused on what you don't like about yourself or your life. The more we focus on the path of others rather than on our own path, we lose control and allow the inner critic to have daily conversations with us keeping us right where it wants us to be. Nowhere. Comparisons deprive us of our joy and diminishes our resiliency. Comparing our lives with others isn't the answer. That doesn't mean we can't find inspiration and learn from others, there is a difference. Each of us are on our own journey in this lifetime. Just because the outside view of your neighbor's house looks quite impressive, doesn't mean that on the inside, they have a place to sit. If you must compare, compare with yourself. We deserve to be the best possible versions of ourselves, not just own selves, but for the benefit and contribution we can give to others.

STEP THREE: LEAN ON YOUR STRENGTHS

Each of were born into this incredible universe with a multitude of special gifts, talents, and interests. Those desires were placed in our hearts before we took our first breath. We all have what we need to grow, thrive, and succeed. The issue is that over time, as we grow older, we sometimes allow the influence of others- our families are a prime example of this phenomenon- to sway us away from our gifts and tell you who it is you should be or ought to be therefore stifling our capacity to expand these gifts. Or, we use them, but not to full capacity. Worse yet, is when we, ourselves ignore our own strengths and dismiss them altogether.

Think of it along these terms. When you were a child, think of the most amazing birthday present you ever received from your parents or those who raised you. Close your eyes and feel what it was like to see that gift and experience the happiness and fulfilment it had to offer you. Your parents were likely just as excited watching you dwell in this space of joy as you explore this gift, played with it, used it, and were grateful for it. If you didn't like it and crossed your arms in protest, scrunched up your face in disgust, and pushed it away, your parents would likely be sad and disappointed that the gift they selected for you was rejected, not appreciated, or never being used. The same goes for God who gifted you with incredible gifts and talents. When you don't use the strengths and gifts that have been given to you, or dismiss them, your actions disappoint Him. When you tap into your gifts, your strengths, He smiles upon you, creating more opportunities, helping you achieve your deepest desires and taking you places you didn't know you could go. When we draw from our strengths in times of uncertainty, we can use our circumstances to be launched into our greatest calling.

By applying these steps, it helps us become stronger to deal with our inner critic. As I mentioned, I don't feel that the inner critic ever goes away, but we can certainly learn how to co-exist with that voice. Several times while writing this book, my inner critic has tried to sneak in on me. *"Who wants to hear what you have to say? How are you going to help someone?"* At which time my voice of reason comes through and responds lovingly to the critic, *"Thank you for your opinion, but I believe my story will help someone."* That gives me a sense of peace and purpose to keep moving forward with my intentions.

It's natural to feel overwhelmed from the fear we experience during hard times. Having strength is one thing but maintaining that mental strength over time is crucial to your comeback. We have a tendency to start out of the gate strong, bouncing right back with a fake smile and, "I got this!" attitude, which is great, but it likely will not last. The important piece to remember is extending our mental strength so that it is maintained through the duration of our darkest moments. Listed below are three simple and effective ways I used during my setback and found them to be very valuable at maintaining my mental strength over time.

Set Goals

Setting goals is a critical piece of maintaining your strength because it provides you with a starting point and an ending point. Setting a goal can be as easy as identifying that you don't want to be where you are at this point. You have identified what you don't want, now let's identify what you do want. That's a goal. Perhaps you can't return to exactly what it is that was lost but look to see if you can set an intention for something like it, or even better. Having no goals is giving up and settling right where you are, which is fine for some, but I'm guessing if you chose to read this book, settling where you are isn't an option for you.

Strive to fulfill your purpose

When we are in transition, the best way to build strength is to be mindful that you are right where you are for a specific purpose. Try to serve that purpose the best you can while you remain patient and faithful for your comeback. Think about what it is that you do well and the gifts you can offer others. As you take a renewed approach in your work, these moves will help shape your path bringing you one step closer to where it is you want to be. Your discoveries may surprise you along the way. You may feel less stress and a renewed passion for your career.

Expend your mental energy wisely

Experiencing a hardship on its own drains your mental energy. If you continue to overanalyze the circumstances that are beyond your control, this will drain your mental energy even quicker. The more mental energy you consume by these thoughts leaves very little left over for creative solutions and ideas to flow through. Conserve your mental energy for productive tasks, such as searching for work that matches your talents, budgeting your money, and setting goals. When your thoughts begin to drift toward those that aren't helpful, make a conscious effort to shift them to more useful matters. The more you make a mindful effort at expending your energy effectively, the more it will become a habit.

Enduring hardships and setbacks in life is inevitable. We are not guaranteed a pain free life, nor are we immune from the harshest blows life gives us. Building strength and leaning on a power greater than you during these times can be your greatest ally. Being strong in itself isn't enough on its own to master resiliency, because at some point, we wear ourselves down and become more vulnerable. When you combine building strength with the other principles in this book, you begin to take back your power so that you too can begin to rise up and become all that you were meant to be.

Recognize and Reflect:

1. In what ways has your inner critic showed up to disrupt your thoughts and deterred you from completing accomplishments? How has that impacted your life or career?

2. What is a new goal you can set for yourself?

3. Describe a way that you can effectively maintain your mental strength during hardships.

*You can't go back and
change the beginning,
but you can start where you are
and change the ending.*

- C.S. Lewis

Chapter Nine

RISE UP: BELIEVE AND BECOME

I once sat on a work committee with a young woman who had a free spirit energy about her. Every meeting that I had with her, she seemed to float into the room with this grand entrance appeal, offering a warm welcome and beautiful smile. The more time we spent together working and collaborating on special projects, the more I took notice that the work flow or suggestions she offered seemed to tilt in her favor, almost as though she was magically paving the way for our committees success. Each time I was in her presence, I would somehow feel inspired to do bigger work. One day, I received an e-mail from her confirming a meeting. Since she wasn't the usual person who scheduled our meetings, her incoming message caught my attention. I opened her message, noting the time and date for our meeting, and as I scrolled down to close out the message, I noticed under her signature line, she had a one line quote that read: *Create the things you wish existed.*

I was intrigued by the statement as I sat there and pondered it for a moment. *Create the things you wish existed.* I took out a scrap piece of paper, wrote it down, and tacked it on my bulletin board over the desk in my office. I had no idea what it meant at the time or why I felt a gentle nudge to write it. In fact, my initial thought as I was writing it and humorously thinking to myself at the same time, *how does one create something that doesn't exist?* Despite my doubt, I listened to my intuition and tacked it on my bulletin board where it stayed for over a year. The day I departed from my corner office for the final time and moved into my cubicle in the middle hallway, I removed it to take with me when it suddenly became clear to me what the intention behind one little sentence meant and how powerful of an impact this one statement would have on my comeback.

When I placed the sticky note that held the intention of wanting to become a leader on my vision board, I didn't know how or when it would happen, as outward circumstances revealed very little to no chance of that happening. I made the decision to turn toward faith and place my trust in something I wasn't able to see, but knew existed. Faith is the ability to know and trust something good will happen. I knew deep within my heart and spirit that something good would come from the circumstances that I was brought to.

After five months of embracing the long wait, I received the phone call I had long been waiting for with excitement. I was offered the management position just days before the Thanksgiving holiday. The elation and joy I felt on top of the happiness I was already enjoying elevated me to a new level of gratitude and appreciation. The Universe wasn't done handing out surprises and abundance quite yet.

Around the time I was offered the supervisor position, another position opened. It was a mid-level management position, with additional responsibility, flexibility, and creativity. I was encouraged to apply and interview, to which I did and again waiting the decision. As I waited for the decision from the interview panel, I was still celebrating my return into leadership and had fully let go of any expectation.

My cell phone rang during our lunchtime office Christmas party less than a week later. It was my new boss. I stepped outside the conference room to accept his call. He was calling to offer me the mid-level manager position. My tummy immediately filled with butterflies. My eyes closed, I smiled, and felt a swell of loving energy surround me, the same loving energy as I felt on the day I stood on the beach, next to the long wooden pier that stretched into the ocean as I watched the sun rise above the horizon. I took a deep breath and said, *"Yes, I absolutely and most graciously accept the position."*

Each of us has the ability to create the life we deserve and bring forth the things we desire. Creating things we want is not an act of selfishness when it's done from a place of love and service. The many wants that I have created over time have been prefaced with the intention of serving. My want to become a leader again was to serve in a role that utilized my skills and gifts while serving others. My want to become a reiki master was to share the light to those around me that needed loving energy. My want to write this book was created with the intention of serving a greater audience providing messages of hope and healing

Being setback doesn't prevent you from connecting with your dreams. Each setback we experience invites us to turn our obstacles into opportunities. American televangelist, Joel Osteen said it best in one of his sermons. We must maintain a bounce back mentality and not stay down in the wake of adversity. The setback is temporary. The setback merely is a setup in which God will pay you back double for your trouble. You will come out better than you were before.

As I finish writing the final chapter, I have taken my time to carefully compose my thoughts as I write, knowing these will be the parting words I leave you with. It has been my heartfelt desire and purpose to write this book for you and in many ways, for me. At times throughout the book, as I revisited some of the stories and composing the reflection questions, it has led me to reflect on why I decided to step forward and share my story. The reason is simple. Our stories connect us and provide great transformation to assist others in times of despair and defeat. By sharing my story with you, my hope is that this has instilled inspiration and encouragement as you reflect on your own circumstances. My comeback is your comeback. My rise from the ashes is your rise. I wrote this book so you wouldn't be alone in your journey and to walk by your side as you embrace your comeback.

My wish is for you to share these messages of hope, healing, and restoration with others that need our light. We choose to meet others when we choose to meet ourselves. The final steps of this book will help you in doing so. Use these steps to reflect on your journey.

STEP ONE: HONOR YOURSELF

Being kind to yourself, knowing that you are enough, just as you are, just as you were meant to be all starts by honoring yourself. You don't have to pretend to be someone you aren't, putting on a smile behind the pain. Difficult situations don't define us. How we respond and continue to behave impacts our ability to build resiliency and comeback quicker and stronger. Give yourself permission to feel the feelings, sitting with them, shedding the emotions in whatever way is helpful, acknowledging what comes up to create space for what lies ahead. Without processing these feelings and not giving yourself a little grace, it can set you back even further, contributing to more delays and increase in frustration with your circumstances. If this does happen, and you find yourself in a place being discouraged, shift your perspective and pray for loving compassion toward yourself. Sometimes it's not about letting go, sometimes it's about letting it be.

STEP TWO: BE WHERE YOU ARE

Where you are is exactly where you need to be right here, right now. It's important to be in the moments that require your attention and presence to help teach you what it is you need to know to transition to the next phase. Even if it is messy and ugly, because it will be and those are exactly the moments we must sit uncomfortably with. When we become too caught up in the destination and not our journey, we cheat ourselves out of some of life's valuable teachings it has to offer.

We gain knowledge, wisdom, insight, and patience from the circumstances that inflict pain and harm on us. Every painful moment not only breaks us, but builds us. Trust in the moment you are in and be where you are being asked to me. This isn't your final destination, just a piece of the journey.

STEP THREE: EMBRACE THE WAIT

Being patient can be difficult. In the moments we grieve the loss of one thing and are uncertain of what is coming next, we rush to fill the void, this sacred space of waiting. We don't realize that this space holds value and meaning as it's a space to be respected It's the passageway between letting go and the arrival of something new. It's a space where healing occurs, we expand, we grow, and learn how capable we are of inventiveness and potential. It's the essence in which we have the opportunity to learn so much about ourselves.

Sitting in the space of wait causes a lot of apprehension. Why? Because it forces us to sit with ourselves being open to vulnerability, insecurity, and uncertainty. It's a space in which we have no choice but to relinquish control and cannot predict the outcome, and we struggle though this notion time and time again. As much as embracing the wait terrifies us, it's also a place where have the ability to feel most alive. Each of us has a fallout. If we can't be with what we need to be with in this place of waiting, that lesson will continue to show up over and over until we sit with it, acknowledge it, grieve it, honor it, and move forward.

The waiting space helps us grow beyond ways we ever could on our own. It's the kind of growth that we witness when we look back on it, having left the lesson behind. It is essential in owning the story of who we are, directing our comeback, contributing to our life in the meaningful manner in which we are destined to go.

STEP FOUR: CREATE THE THINGS YOU WISH EXISTED

You have a unique ability to create the things you wish existed. The only person standing in the way for limitless possibilities, awareness, and potential to emerge for you is you. Even in the midst of chaos and confusion, negative emotions, hard feelings, you still have the ability to find joy, peace, fulfillment, and have FUN in creating the life and career you want. The Universe is unlimited in the abundance it wants to shower upon you, but is waiting on crystal clear intentions from you on what it is you desire and if your thoughts and feelings are in complete alignment with your declarations. When your thoughts and actions come from a place of need, lack, or limitation, these feelings can be blocking the very thing you are attempting to bring forth. Shift your intentions from a mindset of, *"What can I get from this?"* To *"Who can I serve with this?"*

Oftentimes, we wait for others to create the circumstances or opportunities we are hoping for. What if others are doing the same thing and waiting for us? Create the life you want to live. Create the mindset. Create the vision. Write the book. Paint the canvas. Take the trip. Build the home.

We don't have the ability to control the things that happen to us, but we can choose what we take from each of our experiences building strength, resiliency, and faith. We can exercise the power to take back the authority and control over what had control and authority over us. We also can consciously choose to have these experiences be a part of our story of who we are as evidence of the adversity we have conquered that serves as the guiding force behind our comeback.

It is not necessary to be a runner, or a yogi, a master meditator, or reiki practitioner to harness the power of hope and healing. You have all that it takes to turn your setback into your greatest comeback. And when you do, I will be celebrating right along with you, as you root down and rise up.

*Hardships often prepare ordinary people
for extraordinary destiny.*

- C.S. Lewis

ABOUT THE AUTHOR

Kimberly Reid brings her passion for health and wellbeing into the workplace teaching corporate employees mindfulness, meditation, and self-care. As an empowering leader and workshop facilitator, Kim shares her own story to inspire and encourage others on navigating adversity and teaches helpful healing practices. Kim lives in Michigan's Upper Peninsula with her two sons.

You can visit her blog: kimberlydreid.com
Visit her on Facebook: facebook.com/kimberlydawnreid
Find her on Instagram: Instagram.com/kimberlydawnreid

CPSIA information can be obtained
at www.ICGtesting.com
Printed in the USA
FFHW021747261118
49656116-54021FF